BE YOUR PURPOSE

A Ten-Step Journey Through Psychology and Brain Science to the Life You Were Born to Live

DR. SEAN SULLIVAN

BE YOUR PURPOSE

by SEAN SULLIVAN

First Edition December 2015

ISBN 978-0-9834955-7-4 Paperback Edition
978-0-9834955-8-1 Digital Edition

Library of Congress Control Number: 2015905165

Printed in the United States of America

BE YOUR **PURPOSE**

A Ten-Step Journey Through Psychology and Brain Science to the Life You Were Born to Live

Join Dr. Sean Sullivan on an epic adventure

to living out your unique purpose.

FOREWORD

I spent the summer between my first and second years in psychology graduate school in a science-based mindfulness training program. The first question posed in my training was, What do you most fear? Sitting in a room with a group of eager trainees, I quieted my mind as we'd been taught. Then I invited the question in and listened for an answer.

My answer came quickly: "Not living up to my full potential during my life is my greatest fear." In the years since, I've come to see that we each encounter some version of that fear. We fear not fully living up to life. Facing the question of my biggest fear began my training to remove that fear from my life.

What do you fear most?

No matter what it is, fear will live inside you until you are living up to your potential. Fear comes from not knowing what living up to your potential means and, so, not knowing how to consistently hear your personal path of purpose. When you hear your purpose, fear disintegrates. Then, you begin your life as an unceasing revelation along your personal path. That moment of transition is the beginning of true freedom.

For millennia, living masters have taught the specific steps to discovering true freedom from fear. In recent years, brain scientists have clearly demonstrated why the steps work so well. It's my honor to guide you through the steps that I have traversed on my own and shared with many patients, clients, and do-it-yourselfers. I'm thrilled to begin this adventure with you.

Sean

CONTENTS

PROLOGUE

Everything changed in an instant; that's how it happened for me. My first visit to Stillness was the most profound experience in my life, and it directed everything that followed—up to (and perhaps especially) writing this book.

This book is about two journeys: my own winding trek to Stillness, and your first trip there. Together, we will relive my wandering years. Not because they were perfect, but in fact because they weren't. I had spent years mired in the pain of lost love. I was angry, isolated, confused, and disappointed—in the world and in myself.

And then, one lonely night, I pulled an old guitar onto my lap. I plucked a string to wash away my thoughts with sound. The vibration moved through me; the reverb expanded into the room. I closed my eyes and listened with my whole being. I let go of everything and followed the waning hum. Quieter, softer, quieter, quieter . . . finally into nothing.

Unintentionally, unknowingly, I had crossed the line into Stillness. Questions ceased. I could look at, listen to, drink from timeless, placeless nowhere. Minutes later, I returned. And I was changed. But I didn't know how to return to Stillness. I didn't even know where I'd gone, or how, or why. I only knew that I wanted—*needed*—to return. So I searched high and low. From an urban classroom to the jungle, I crossed the globe and sought out masters. I learned everything I could about psychology and brain science. I became a therapist and a teacher.

Over time, I gained a deep understanding of what I'd experienced. I was able to retrace my path to and from Stillness and to distill it into the journey you will now undertake—the second journey in this book.

But your trip will be smoother because you have an experienced companion alongside you. I am with you for every step. My mistakes and successes become your launching point, and together we will create your map to Stillness. Together we will embark on your own epic journey to. . .

BE YOUR PURPOSE

Think of this book as your travel guide on a great adventure. A traditional travel guide teaches you what you need to know for a successful journey. *Be Your Purpose* provides you with the tools to make a successful journey to Stillness and living as your life purpose. But unlike a vacation to a far-off land, this is a visit that you will make again and again to a place you cannot touch. And the goal isn't a scrapbook of memories, but a deep connection to your life purpose.

But what does that mean? What *is* "life purpose"? You are your life purpose when you are able to clearly hear and take the next best step in your life. In terms that are both simplest and the most grand, it's the life you were born to live. It's the life that gives you the most fulfillment, the greatest joy. It's *being* your purpose.

A journey to your life purpose begins by learning to consciously navigate your inner world—the world that exists inside a person's brain and body. This ability enables you to intentionally change the function of your own brain cells, access expanded states of mind and body, and deepen your insight into the nature of life. In other words, being able to connect to your inner world in specific ways lets you connect to, know, and become your life purpose.

For centuries, however, developing this connection was limited to specially trained or uniquely gifted masters. Such people spent years learning to discipline their minds to navigate their inner worlds. Brain science was far behind, with little research-based data.

Today, I have a map that I am eager to share. I have a science-based process to aid in its navigation. Visiting Stillness is now available to anyone who can complete the ten-step process of *Be Your Purpose.*

Stillness is no longer an impenetrable mystery. Let's journey there together.

CONNECTING TO SILENCE

On my first visit to Stillness, I didn't understand the science, psychology, or inner world mastery tools. However, I gained personal experience with something huge: Silence.

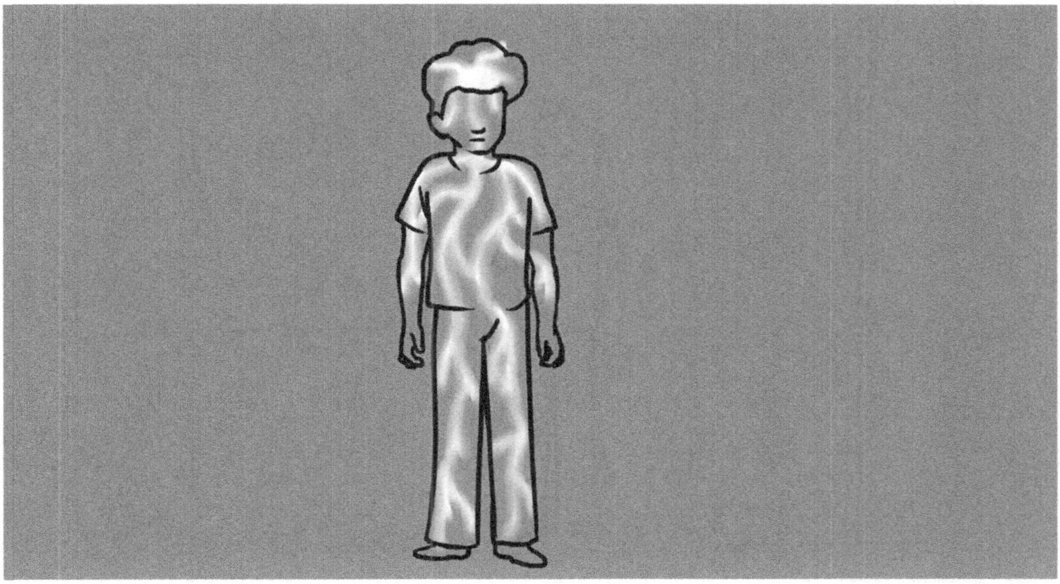

The silent energy of life infuses all of us, at all times.

Silence is what I call the silent energy of life, which is always flowing from Stillness. The Ten Steps to Stillness guide you to connecting to Silence and following it to Stillness.

Connecting to Silence sounds simple, but it isn't always. You may forget your destination or that following Silence will lead you there. You may even forget the fact that you're on a journey. But with the Ten Steps, you will be able to control and deepen your connection strategically.

As your connection to Silence and self-awareness deepens, you can navigate closer to Stillness. Visiting Stillness is how you become flooded by, and thus consistently aware of, Silence. When you can visit intentionally, you can learn to guide Silence as it unfolds through you. That's how you uncover and become your purpose.

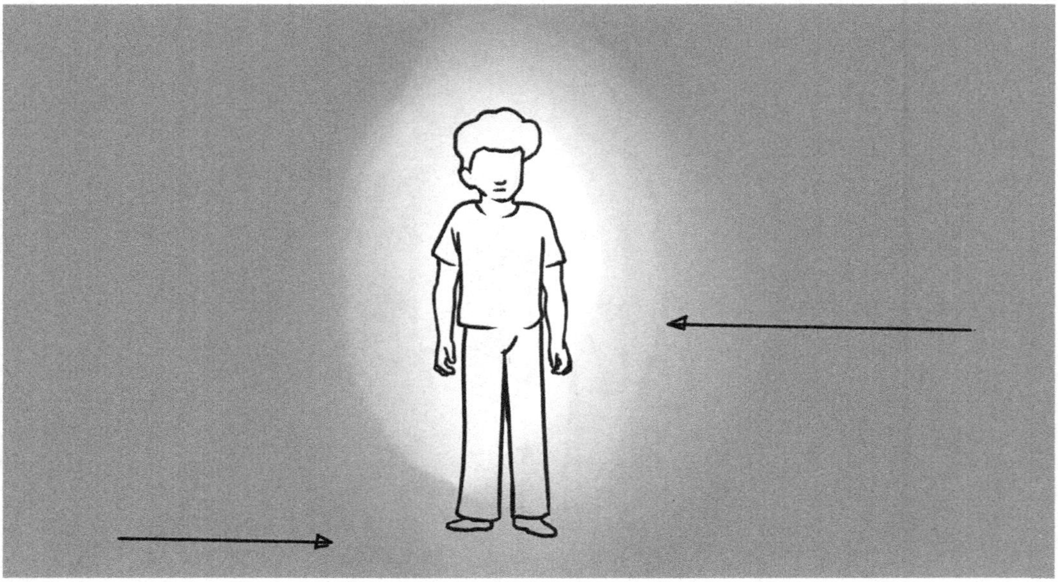

Being consistently aware of the Silence flowing through you means being able to precisely align with the life you were born to live. It means being your purpose.

THE FEAR OF INNER QUIET

Your biggest obstacle on this adventure won't be something you can easily move, however. It will be yourself. Visiting Stillness frequently over the years taught me about a hidden challenge: the instinctual fear of experiencing a silent inner world that we all share, until you overcome it with practice.

Our brains are programmed to keep us feeling safe, so our fears are frequently cloaked in distraction. Rather than encounter inner quiet, we keep an incessant conversation inside our heads. This is us unconsciously disguising our fears. Rather than moving through the fear toward Stillness, we tend to drown out its call with a noisy, distracting, inner life.

Inner noise only reinforces fear over time. Distraction can also increase anxiety, isolation, loneliness, anger, and a sense of disconnection. Visiting Stillness, on the other hand, dissolves all these and infuses your life with peace, health, and meaning.

A HEALING JOURNEY

Even after just one visit to Stillness, I knew that my failure to notice the silent life flowing through me was a major obstacle on my path of healing. My first visit introduced me to the immense powers of strategically connecting Silence. It is the most precious gift I have ever received.

I want to pass the gift of visiting Stillness to you.

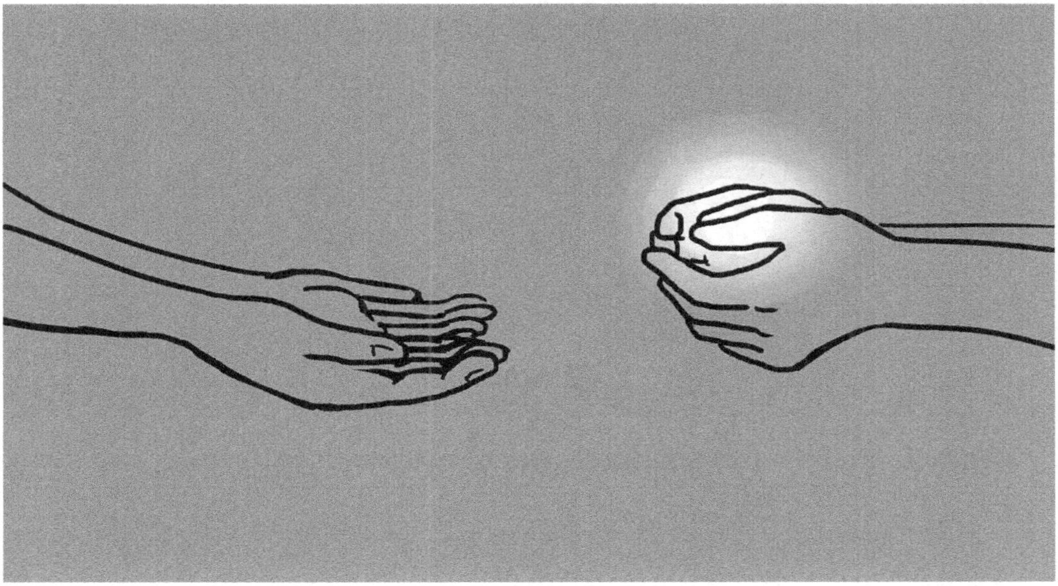

When I think back to that first visit, I remember what came before. I remember the pain, the loneliness, the longing and the anger. I remember how stuck, lost and frustrated I felt. And I'll walk through those times with you, so that you can share my journey just as I share yours.

But, even more importantly, I remember learning that life is ever flowing through each of us. I remember how this key insight led to discovering and learning how to be my purpose.

I dedicated my life to creating a scientifically based process that ensured consistent contact with and ongoing awareness of Silence. In the years since, I began guiding others to Stillness. And yet, for all of us, a consistent awareness of Silence doesn't come until we have visited Stillness repeatedly.

Finding a path, building your map and being able to visit Stillness when you choose is a life-changing journey. I want to share that journey with you.

Ready to make a life-changing journey through your inner world?

Let's go . . .

JOURNEY PREPARATION

LAUNCHING OUR JOURNEY

If you've ever read a travel guide, you know that its advice applies even *before* you leave your front door. What should you pack? Do you need any special clothing or equipment? What's the best way to get there? Do you need to understand any important phrases or cultural mores? What are the must-see sights, and how can I find them?

Your itinerary to Stillness may look different than a tour company's travel guide, but preparation is just as important—and actually very similar. In this preparation section, Part I focuses on how you can plan your trip and Part II helps you understand what to expect when you get there.

I like to envision our journey preparation as a conversation from my psychology office in San Francisco. This is where I walk my patients through the Ten Steps to Stillness. You'll learn how to efficiently connect to Silence whenever you choose.

Connecting to Silence in your inner world is the foundation of the Ten Steps to Stillness. It also was the launching point of my own epic adventure around the world. Step 1 and Step 2 help you master the tools you need to navigate your inner world, including your first Mind Exercise and the Daily Ritual. Beginning in Step 3, we'll travel to locations where the key brain research, psychological insights, and inner world practices first occurred or are widely in use today—the places I traveled as I wrote *Be Your Purpose.*

Each step toward Stillness and each leg of our trip will unlock more of life's mysteries. You'll uncover your purpose, find your peace, and live out your joy. In the end, you'll take Step 10 and enter Stillness.

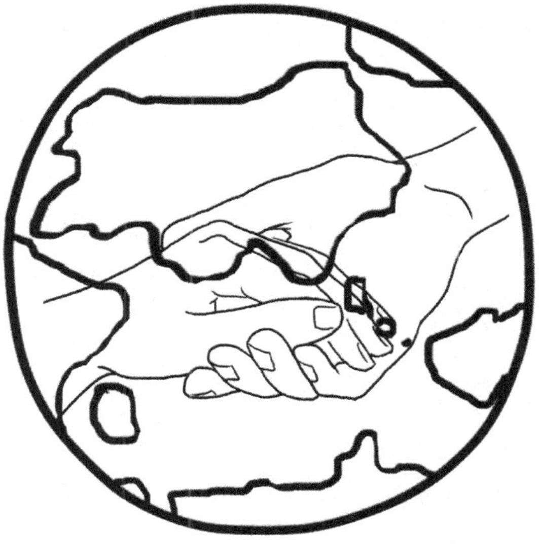

You have begun a remarkable adventure.

PART I:

GETTING READY FOR THE ADVENTURE

As your companion and guide, I want to make sure that you set out on your adventure prepared for success. What do you need to do and know before we begin? I like to think of this section as the three Ps: pacing, packing, and pitfalls.

PACING

How long will this journey take? How do we travel? We can't reach Stillness in a car or an airplane—but we can reach it, and dependably, by completing the Ten Steps.

Thanks to years of retracing and refining my own path, the Ten Steps to Stillness are simple to follow. After you complete Step 1, you're ready for Step 2, and so on. Each step should take less than one hour to complete.

To get the maximum benefit from your journey, I recommend the following guidelines:

1. Progress through the Ten Steps at your chosen pace. Don't rush, and don't worry. This is not a race.
2. Set aside time for at least five minutes of physical exercise before you begin each step, starting in Step 3. You'll learn more about this as you read.

3. If you prefer, you can watch (not read) your Daily Ritual and Mind Exercises as you encounter them throughout your journey. Video versions are available at BeYourPurpose.com.

PACKING

What tools or equipment do we need to take with us? No responsible guidebook would tell someone to fly to a foreign country without detailing the necessary visas, or to embark on a roadtrip without mentioning the need for a reliable vehicle and emergency supplies. None of your tools for our journey will fit in a luggage compartment, but they're essential all the same.

Perhaps the most essential "item" is one that we will refine together as we journey together: a map. Unlike a usual trip, you won't be able to look at the complete map until after you visit Stillness—following Silence through the Ten Steps will fill in the details of your map. Similarly, a deep understanding of Stillness comes into focus only after you complete your journey. Meantime, you can "hold on" to the elemental truth that Silence flows from Stillness.

Another important tool is emotional visualization, a recent brain science discovery. *Emotional visualization* means consciously processing emotional content in your imagination. A wide range of new research has empirically demonstrated that it changes how we experience our emotional lives.

Think of the power of visualization techniques used by trainers, athletes, performers, and others in skills-based arenas. For generations, these people have visualized improved performance in order to achieve it. And it works—for skills *and* emotions. Visualizing a skill produces brain changes that result in more efficient performances of the skill. Similarly, emotional visualization recruits more brain cells to feel and express the visualized emotion. In other words, if you visualize "loving," more brain cells will become associated with actually *feeling* "loving."

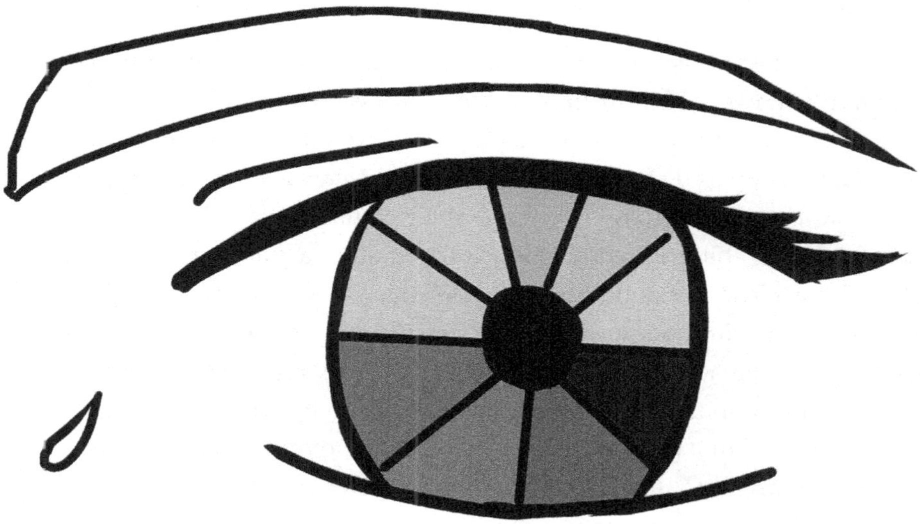

Emotional visualization actually changes your brain, allowing you to take control of your path through your inner world.

One of the ways that you will use this tool is through Mind Exercise. Mind Exercises are directed meditations that increase your attention span, improve your focus, and grow your inner world power by strategically sculpting your brain. Think of a Mind Exercise as analogous to physical exercise. Just as physical exercise improves your body's strength and function in targeted ways, Mind Exercises improve the strength and function of your attention in targeted ways. And just as physical exercise changes your musculature and endurance, Mind Exercises change your brain's structure and your psychological and emotional state.

Finally, you'll need to pack commitment. It's easier to "go home" on this journey than a physical one—sometimes too easy. I want you to make a commitment to yourself to deepen your awareness of and your sensitivity toward your inner world. Pay close attention to what you are experiencing inside your brain and body, applying what you learn throughout *Be Your Purpose.* New paths will be revealed, and you'll be able to experience a dimension of life you could not before. But this will only happen with commitment, even in the face of doubt.

PITFALLS

One of the scariest parts (and one of the most exhilarating parts, too) of travel is the unknown. If you can take your first step to Stillness with less fear, you will be more successful. One way to accomplish that is to warn you about the most common obstacles, so you are prepared. Throughout *Be Your Purpose*, I'll share stories of how I and other inner world travelers have overcome their challenges.

The best and worst thing about the obstacles is that they are all you. Because it's your inner world, it all flows from, to, and within you. On your journey, you will gain greater access to and control of your inner world. As you step towards that confident and consistent access, however, you may unintentionally attempt to block your own way.

The most common pitfall is forgetting the journey that you are on—the journey to Stillness. You'll notice that, just as it's easy to forget the oxygen you must breathe, it's easy to forget the ongoing flow of Silence that animates you. Remember, you follow Silence to Stillness. Forgetting Silence means losing track of where you are going. Also, the cells in your brain become more vulnerable to stress, and rediscovering Silence becomes harder.

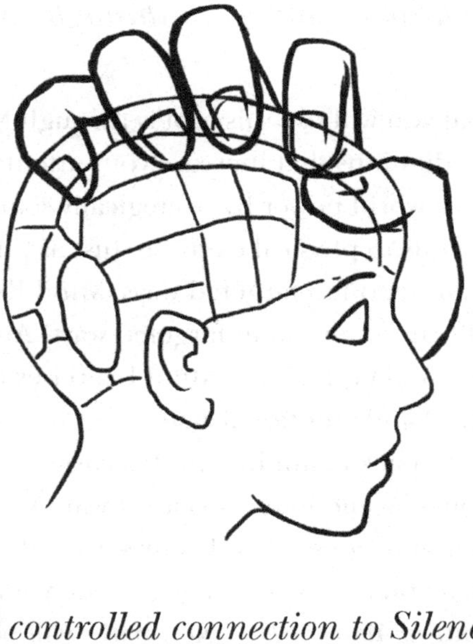

A conscious and controlled connection to Silence that reduces damaging stress can be achieved through Mind Exercise.

Staying connected to Silence is an act of emotional and physical healing that also enables you to navigate your inner world. Because it's easy to forget, I'll repeatedly remind you that our journey follows Silence to Stillness. Do your best to hold on to this idea. It will help you build your map.

Another common pitfall is the simple art of distraction. The Ten Steps to Stillness take you through your inner world—the world inside your brain and body through which Silence flows. Noise within the inner world will challenge you throughout your journey; its distortions will distract you from consistently recognizing and remaining connected to the Silence flowing through you each moment. Being distracted from Silence can provoke feelings of alienation, isolation, and unquenchable desire—causing you to fall off the strategic path to your life purpose.

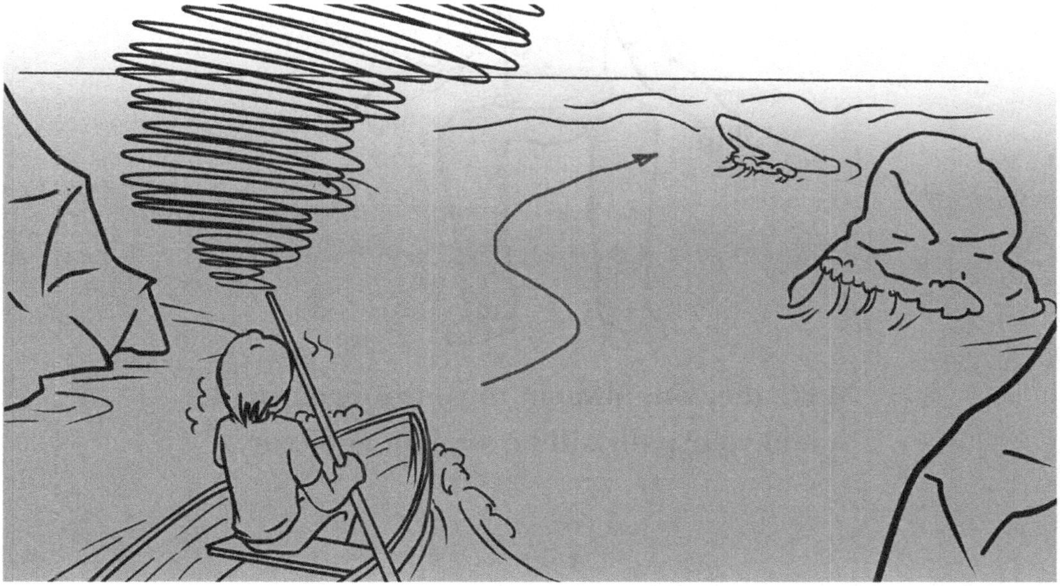

Distractions from your inner noise can prevent you from navigating a strategic path through your inner world.

This noise, however, comes entirely from you. Do you remember the fear of Stillness I mentioned a few pages ago? We cope with this fear by maintaining an incessant chatter in our heads. Inner noise encourages you to forget about Silence—to avoid obstacles by simply ignoring the path altogether.

To remain consistently connected to Silence, you'll observe precisely how *your* inner noise distracts *your* awareness. You'll master strategies that ensure you notice when your connection to Silence is threatened, and you'll learn to habitually reconnect to Silence.

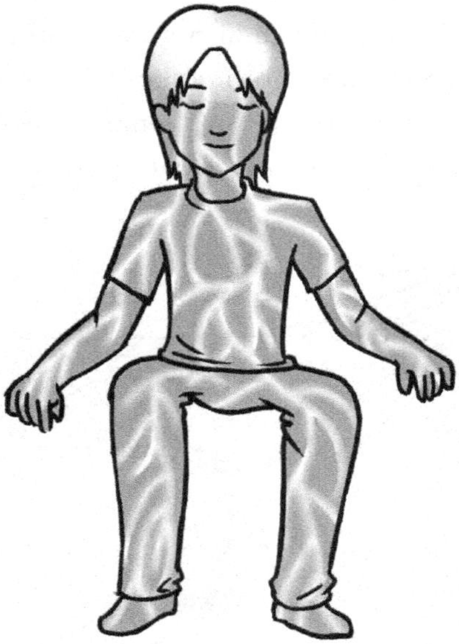

Make the commitment to your journey now, and your path will be straight and true.

PART II:

HOW IT WORKS "INSIDE" YOU

The inner world is unlike any place you've ever visited. It is within you. It *is* you. And yet, it's a part of you that you may have never been truly in touch with. This section will help you understand what you will encounter: a sort of primer on how your inner world works and what you'll "see."

THE LANGUAGE OF THE INNER WORLD

You probably have heard the phrase *inner dialogue* before: a term for the conversation that takes place inside your head each moment. Recent scientific breakthroughs have taught us new things about the language of the inner world. Your inner dialogue is actually much more than words passing through your brain.

Your inner world is constantly processing impulses, feelings, sensations, memories, images, metaphors, and all other information from the outer world (i.e., the world outside your brain and body). Without any effort, your vast intelligence synthesizes all of this ongoing communication into a language-based narrative—your inner dialogue.

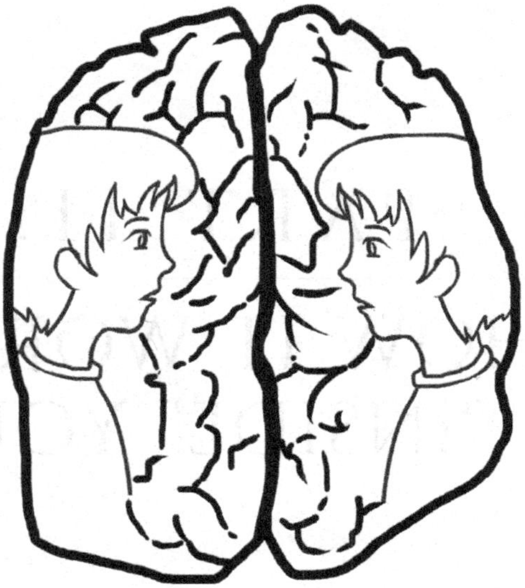

Your inner dialogue is the ongoing communication of all the activity in your inner world each moment.

Your inner world translation skills developed from the conversational patterns, tones, and attitudes you absorbed while growing up. As you accumulate experiences throughout your life, both good and bad, the way you process your inner dialogue continues to evolve.

A patient of mine, Jim, provides an interesting sidebar to this—one that is unusual, even to me. Jim is deaf. He was understandably perplexed when I asked him to "listen" to his thoughts. I asked him to describe how he observes the thoughts that run through his mind, and he explained that he "reads" them. His brain found the most efficient way to process information using the tools he had.

This anecdote is important because your brain will do the same as Jim's: It will use the best tools for *you*. Some people "listen to" their thoughts, some people "read," and some people "see" them. Some people do all three.

In fact, almost all of us process inner dialogue by painting scenes within our heads—creating an inner movie. Here's an example: Imagine yourself smelling a red rose. Can you "see" this in your mind? If so, you are watching a scene of your inner movie. Throughout your journey, you will hone your ability to see your inner movie more clearly.

Your inner dialogue produces a story in your head—a set of scenes that create your emotional experience.

Your inner movie, which is really just the story that your inner dialogue writes for you, dictates your emotions. The content of your inner dialogue defines what you are visualizing, and the scenes (like your inner dialogue) are generally repetitive. If you feel at peace right now, you are likely to feel at peace tomorrow as well.

To intentionally plot a strategic course through Silence to Stillness, you will take time each day to observe your inner dialogue and, in time, watch your inner movie. As you complete the Ten Steps to Stillness, you'll bring each moment more fully into your awareness.

CHANGING YOUR INNER WORLD

Once you become aware of the moment-to-moment conversation that you're translating in your head, you can use emotional visualization to make strategic changes in your inner world and navigate to your life purpose. You'll also see that even when your inner dialogue is operating on autopilot, its ongoing flow is training your future emotional life. Even if you aren't aware of the content of your inner dialogue at any moment, it is always changing your inner world by reshaping the way your actual brain cells interact.

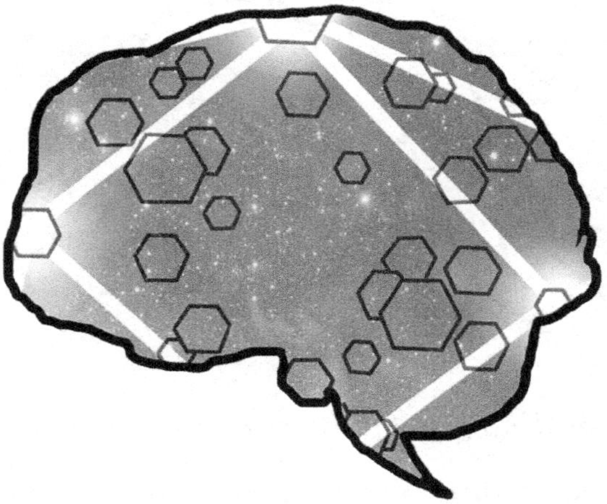

Your inner dialogue changes your brain's structure and function.

Remember, your inner movie tends to repeat itself. A stressful inner dialogue fosters more stress because it encourages distracting noise in your inner world. Stressful inner dialogue also actually damages your brain cells by exposing them to the harmful chemicals related to stress. Additionally, it becomes easier and easier to fall prey to these damaging distractions each time they go unchecked.

Conversely, when you can access and direct your inner dialogue, you can deepen your connection to Silence. Then you can create strategic emotional visualizations, which allow you to intentionally change the behavior of millions of your brain cells.

You'll be able to sculpt your brain as you choose. By doing so, you will physically, emotionally, spiritually, and practically *become* your purpose.

Such strategic changes take time and effort. After all, it involves inner world practices that previously were only available to those who spent decades in pursuit of mastery. By following the Ten Steps the strategic changes you make will anchor into the cells of your brain and body to produce consistent changes in your life.

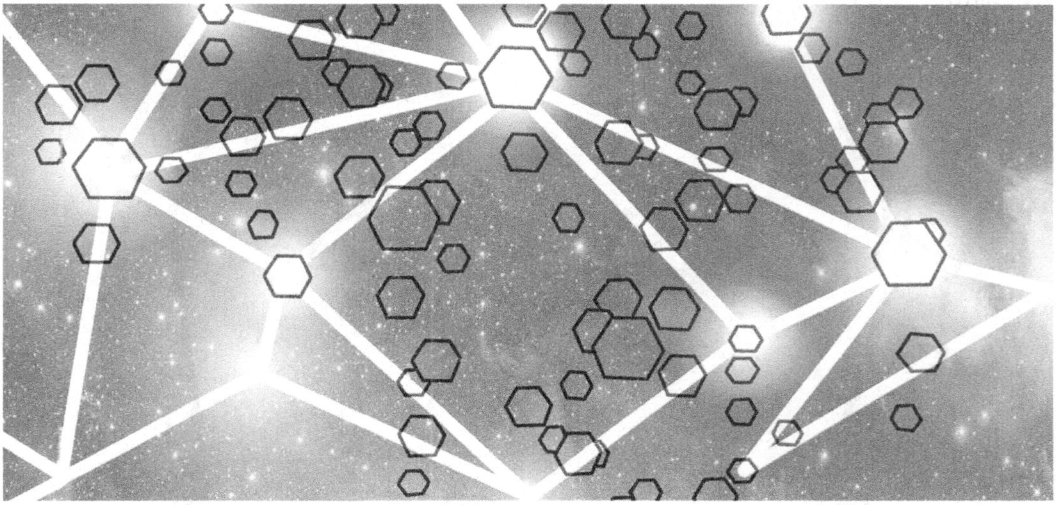

Changed cells equate to a changed life.

MILESTONES ALONG YOUR JOURNEY

In fact, the changes you will experience are among the most important "sights" along the way. With the knowledge you gain about inner dialogue's connection to how your future unfolds and about Silence's power to align you with your life purpose, you can ask and answer key questions that reveal where you are along your journey to Stillness at any moment.

- How natural and easy is it for you to experience Silence flowing through you?
- How natural and easy is it for you to become aware of the content of your arising inner dialogue?

- How natural and easy is it for you to quiet the translation of your inner dialogue?

Each of the Ten Steps will give you practice applying the new brain science to navigate and master your unique inner journey. You'll take full ownership of directing how Silence flows through you. After you visit Stillness, you'll answer each of the questions above as an inner world master would.

Your experience of life will change, and it will be one of the most beautiful and powerful things you will ever "see."

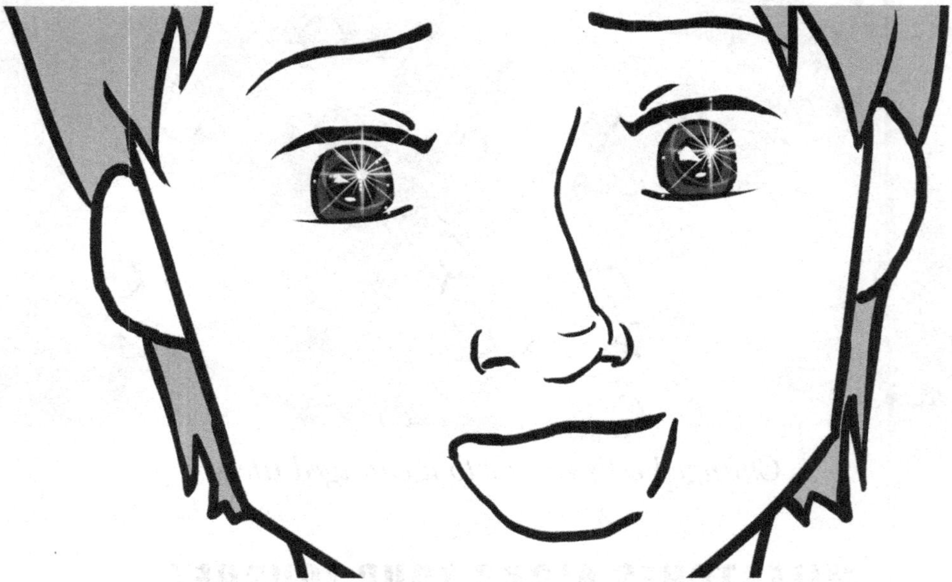

You will be amazed.

LANDMARK OF THE INNER WORLD

Yet even in the inner world, there are some things to look for that will almost feel as if they are outside yourself. The most important of these is the Bridge of Translation.

The Bridge of Translation is a metaphorical bridge that connects your inner world to the outer world. It is one of the most crucial features of the inner world. It has the power to reveal your life purpose; it can shape your personal experience and expression of life each moment.

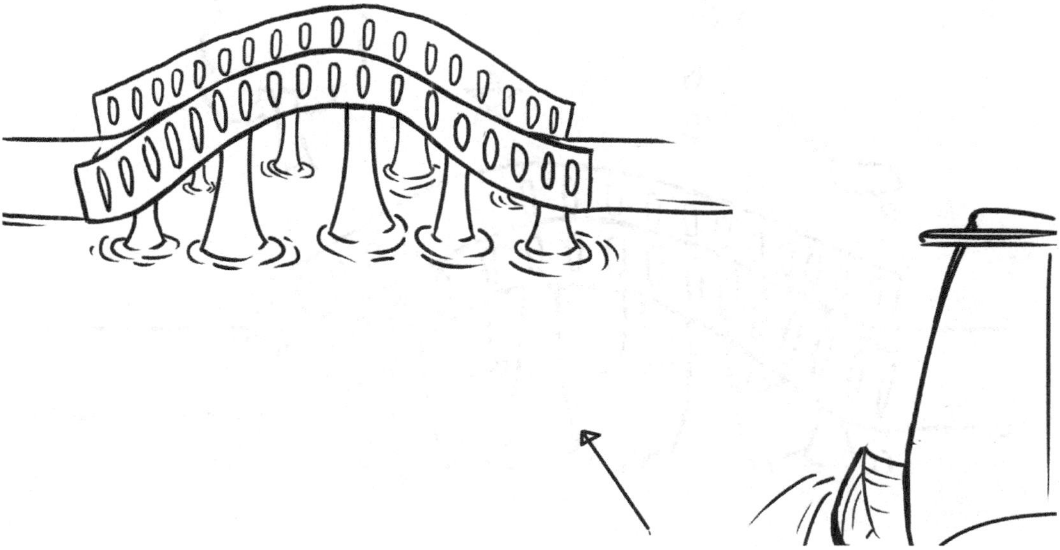

But how? Think of a well-built, effectively maintained real world bridge. Bridges can perform multiple functions to improve lives of the people who use them—facilitating the flow of traffic, connecting previously disconnected locations, regulating access between these locations, providing people increased freedom of movement, opening up new life opportunities. The Bridge of Translation also serves multiple purposes—facilitating the flow of information between inner and outer worlds, translating the high-speed travel, giving your instincts and emotions a voice, allowing your inner world to adjust to the ever-changing external environment, and providing you with a consistent sense of identity. All of these influence how your inner world functions and, so, how you experience life.

All of your life experience comes through the Bridge of Translation, regardless of your awareness. Its influence on how you experience life cannot be overstated.

The Bridge of Translation is in constant use because the interaction between your inner world and outer world is always in flux. It's like high-speed traffic flowing in two directions. The bridge translates messages that originate within your body into thought, emotion, sensation, and instinct. It simultaneously takes outer world stimuli and translates them into information your inner world can respond to and synthesize.

Once the translation of both streams of information is complete, in another feat of genius, your bridge allows for a conversation between the two silent languages: that produced from information inside your body and that produced from information outside your body. This conversation is unending. The two streams of information collide, converse, and combine into your inner movie flowing above your Bridge of Translation—revealing the story of your life each moment.

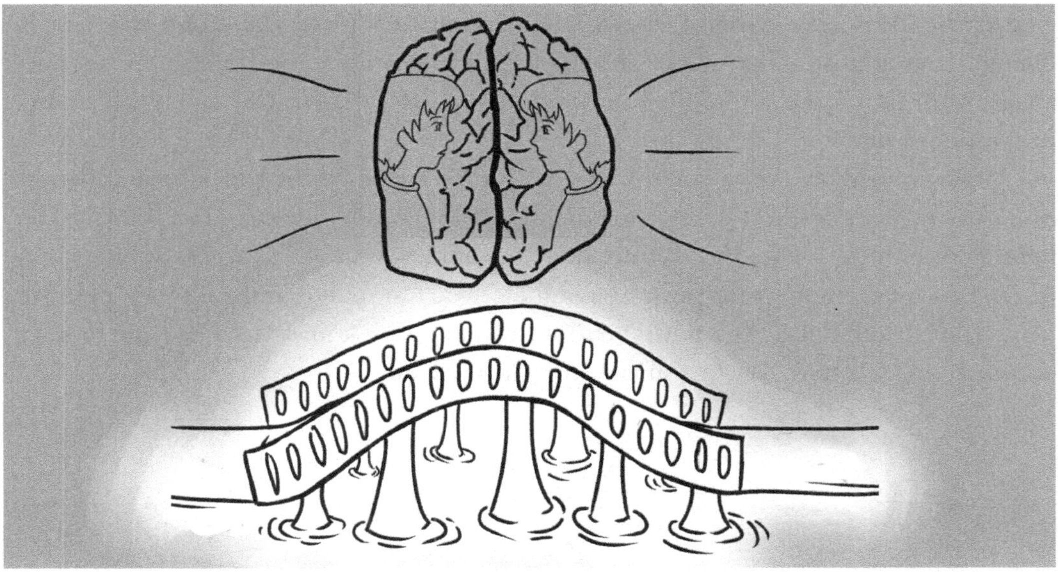

When you listen closely, as you will learn to do as you move through the Ten Steps to Stillness, you can also hear your bridge translating what matters to you into language. With each visit, you'll become more adept at using the bridge to allow for strategic access to your inner dialogue.

THE JOURNEY'S UNENDING REWARDS

Together, we will walk through a precise process of entering and embracing the inner world. You'll see how I made my slow trek from initial, intermittent awareness of Silence to fully embracing and eventually directing Silence flowing through me to be my purpose. Steadying myself through practice opened my heart to knowing that life is overflowing through me each moment. If you complete your journey, you too will be rewarded a thousand times over.

You will know exactly how to be your life purpose.

When you become consistently and intimately aware of Silence flowing through your particular combination of DNA and stored personal history, and of the inner dialogue that it produces, you deeply experience how unique *and* interconnected we all are. Your inner journey and life purpose will be individual to you, but it will change the world we share.

By employing your personal strengths and recent scientific breakthroughs about inner world practices, you'll move through the Ten Steps to Stillness. You will learn to habitually know and direct your inner dialogue and, eventually, to access Stillness and be your purpose. Being your purpose is a lifelong achievement and a lifelong practice.

You have the map. You have the tools. You have the knowledge. It's time to start on the Ten Steps, to make the journey of your inner life.

Let's go!

STEP 1

Making the One Small Change

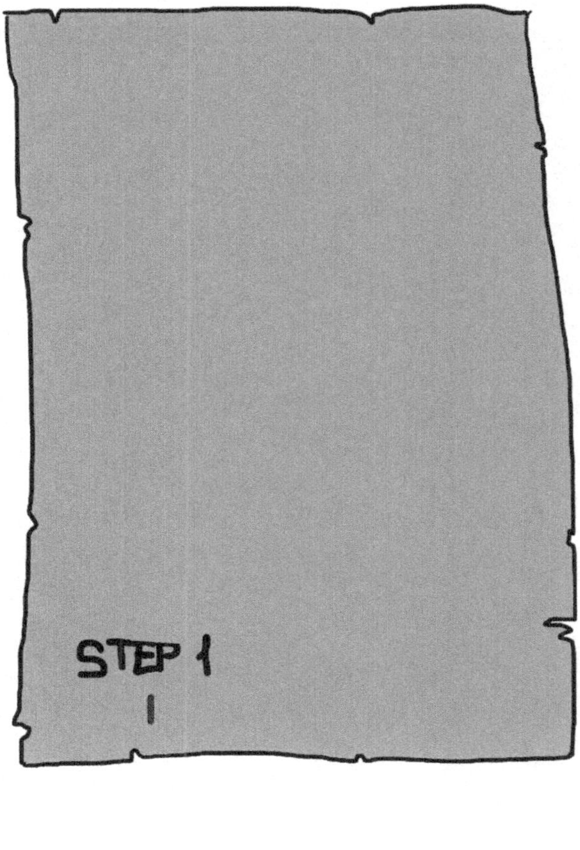

STEP 1: MAKING THE ONE SMALL CHANGE

The real voyage of discovery consists not in seeking new landscapes, but in having new eyes.

— Marcel Proust

Years before my first visit to Stillness, I lost the first true love of my life. "I just don't love you anymore," my girlfriend said through tears. We'd spent our college years in the unparalleled world of young love, and I was crushed. A more painful sentence could not exist.

For months afterward, I couldn't function. I woke each morning to a gnawing pain in my stomach that reminded me of my loss. The pain would expand into my chest. As the day wore on, it would become harder and harder to breathe. I needed help.

My desperation trumped old prejudices, and I made a therapy appointment at the college health center. The therapist listened to me for forty-five minutes, and told me that a broken heart was like a broken leg—both needed time to heal properly. I liked hearing that; I felt a glimmer of hope.

Then, she told me that her next available appointment was in two weeks. Desperation returned. I couldn't make it that long, and I left in a dark cloud of pain.

Wandering through campus, I told myself I needed change. At that exact moment, I passed a sign: "Meditation Classes." I'd passed that building every day, but today, the sign caught my eye and my desire for relief (or even distraction) from my pain led me to follow it inside.

I heard a teacher speaking through a closed door. I snuck in, ducked a greeting as the teacher smiled at me, and took a seat in the very back. This mere accident of timing led me to the most important life skill I've ever learned: listening to my inner dialogue.

"Close your eyes and follow my voice," the teacher instructed the twenty or so students. "Focus your attention inside your mind. Observe the thoughts that arise, whether you want them to arise or not."

He compared these thoughts to ripples on a body of water: changing and moving, while the deeper waters below remain calm. I focused, and soon I "heard" these ripples of thought, crossing the waters of my mind without my direction.

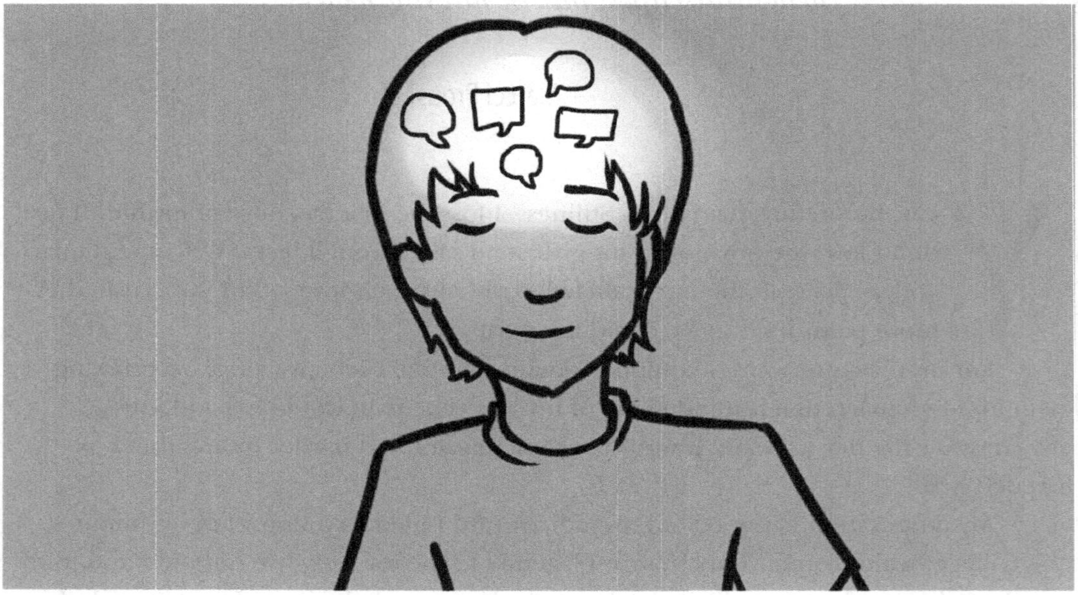

Without my conscious participation, ripples of thought splashed onto the surface of the waters of my mind.

In fact, many of the same thoughts returned again and again. "Why can't you just get her back?" "Can't you solve your own problems?" "Does this guy even know what he's talking about?"

The realization of this repetition startled me out of the moment, but it taught me something huge: We all have an inner dialogue that often repeats itself.

THE ONE THOUGHT

Some inner dialogue repetitions are fleeting, related to the experience of the moment, but we've all had one version of repeating inner dialogue that repeats for a large portion of our lives, perhaps in its entirety. I call this *the persistent inner dialogue.*

Most often, persistent inner dialogue is sparked by a particular sentence or idea. I call this the One Thought, and it almost always boils down to something like this:

"I am not consistently living the purposeful life I want to live."

This statement usually is cloaked in your own life and personal challenges. For example, you may hear one of the following questions: "What am I meant to do with my life?" "Why don't I do the thing I know I should be doing to pursue my dreams?" "Why don't I have a dream I want to pursue?" "Why am I always getting in my own way instead of accomplishing something meaningful?"

Perhaps you hear specific questions about the way you're living: "Should I stay in this relationship?" "Should I have kids?" "Should I go back to school?" "What's the best career path for me now?" "Why do I feel so anxious all the time?" "Why don't I kick this unhealthy habit (like overeating, over-drinking, over-drugging, or over-anything-else-ing)?"

Perhaps you simply hear condemnations and criticisms of yourself. "I am doing a horrible job." "I will never be good enough." "I'm too stupid (or lazy or unlovable or controlling or…) to ever do anything useful." "I can't do anything right." "I don't deserve anything more."

Your persistent inner dialogue may be on infinite repeat, reinforcing negative emotions in your entire brain and body.

Almost all of us confront thoughts like these related to our life purpose. Even though the questions are different on the outside, they are all variations on the One Thought:

"I am not consistently living the purposeful life I want to live."

The reality is that so many of us wake up and/or fall asleep to the One Thought. Since we can't easily address it, we try to push the One Thought out of our minds. It always returns, though. The One Thought demands attention.

When you pay close attention to the One Thought, you notice that it does not exist on its own. It is the beginning of a sequence of thoughts—the persistent inner dialogue. It goes something like this. First, the One Thought arises:

"I am not consistently living the purposeful life I want to live."

The One Thought has put your persistent inner dialogue into motion—like a pebble in water causes ripples to propagate outward. It might start out positive:

"I need to make a change. I know I can do it."

But doubt and ambivalence creep in as your persistent inner dialogue continues:

"I've failed before though."

"I guess, if I'm being honest, I'm not really sure I can do it."

Soon enough, the persistent inner dialogue circles back on itself, returning to the One Thought:

"I'm not sure I can consistently live the purposeful life I want to live."

You're right back where you started, repeating and reinforcing the One Thought and its negative emotions.

The crazy part is that persistent inner dialogue is just an old brain habit—what your mind has become conditioned to repeat over the years—yet it has enormous power and control over your life. If your persistent inner dialogue reinforces the illusion that you cannot live as you want to, it can block you from ever encountering Silence. It can keep you from following Silence to Stillness and living out your life purpose.

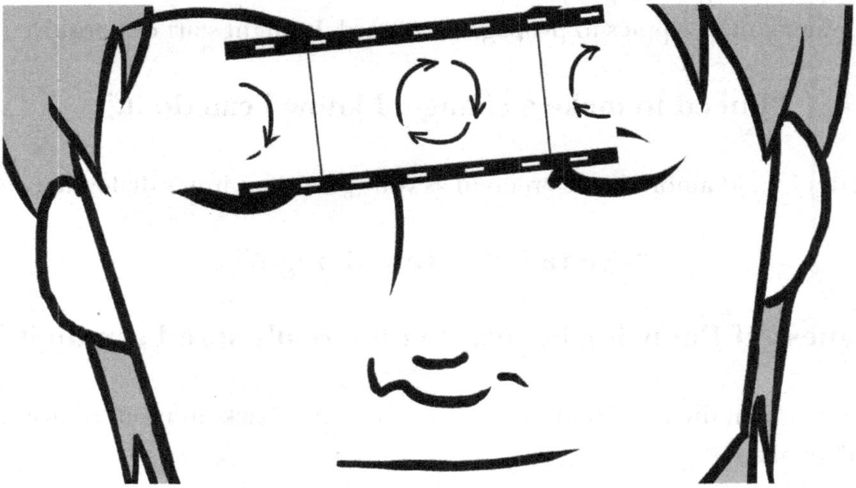

The persistent inner dialogue can sabotage your emotional life.

No matter how ingrained this brain habit is, however, there is hope. And it starts simply by giving the One Thought the attention that it craves. Listen closely to your persistent inner dialogue, and you will become intimately aware that you are making a choice during the brief time that Silence flows through you. You are choosing your reality, and you can choose to make it as beautiful as you want to be. All you need to do is shift one thing about the way you see reality.

THE ONE SMALL CHANGE

Step 1 is making the One Small Change to your persistent inner dialogue. It really is small, but it opens the floodgates for Silence to flow and enable you to make your journey to Stillness and achieve massive lifestyle changes.

I have seen over and over with my patients that if you address the One Thought, you are also addressing all of your questions about your personal path of purpose. It's the first step to a life of consciously choosing awareness of the silent life that flows through you.

Here's how you make the One Small Change:

First, invite your persistent inner dialogue to begin as it typically does. Silently say the One Thought to yourself, and allow it to unfold as it usually does:

"I am not consistently living the purposeful life I want to live."

"I need to make a change. I know I can do it."

Don't stop. Allow the doubt and ambivalence to unfold:

"I've failed before though."

"I guess, if I'm being honest, I'm not really sure I can do it."

"I'm not sure I can consistently live the purposeful life I want to live."

Okay. Now here's the One Small Change. Ready? Add the following sentence to the end:

"I'm learning exactly how people who have navigated their inner world to become their purpose did it, and I'm following in their footsteps, step by step."

Every time—*every time*—you have doubts about whether this journey to Stillness will work for you, I want you to complete your persistent dialogue with the One Small Change. Do this throughout the Ten Steps to Stillness. That's it.

WHY IT WORKS: THE BRAIN-BODY CONNECTION

The One Small Change works because, each time, you intentionally trigger what's popularly known as the brain-body connection. Recent brain science discoveries have revealed that your brain and your body are more than simply connected. Your thoughts change your brain and your body the instant they occur. On the most fundamental level, your brain and your body are the same thing.

Take a moment to digest that idea. Your brain is your body. Your body is your brain. Changing your body is changing your brain, and changing your brain is changing your body. Your journey to Stillness truly begins in this moment, when you realize that your brain *is* your body.

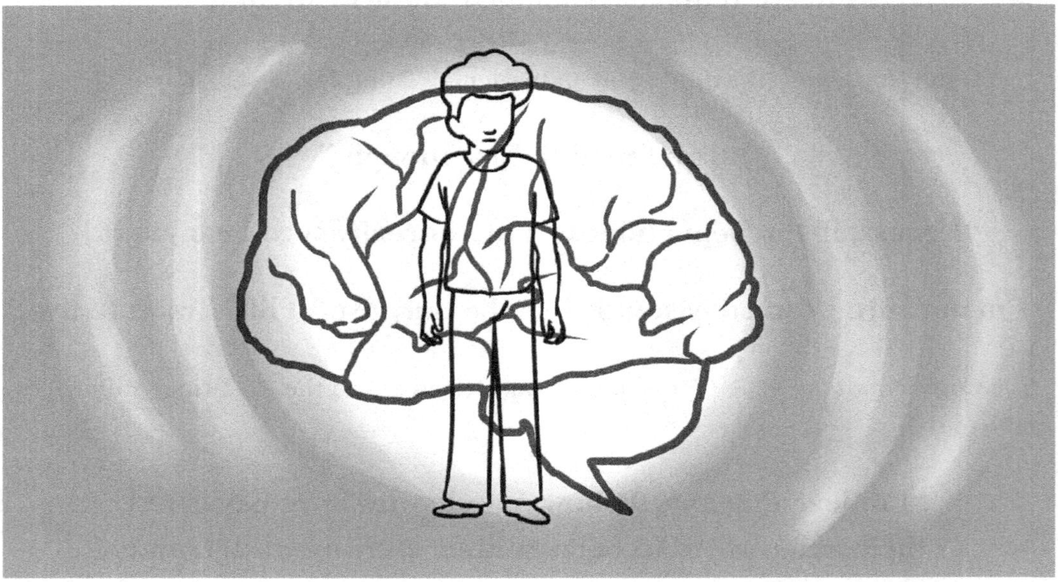

Your brain and your body are not just connected. They are the same.

When you make intentional inner world changes like the One Small Change, the cells in your brain and body immediately change too. That's why knowing how to change your inner world is knowing how to change your body. Knowing how to change your inner world is knowing how to change your life too.

Making the One Small Change affirms your belief in your ability to complete your journey to Stillness and discover your life purpose. It begins the process of learning how to navigate your inner world, so you can make strategic changes. The One Small Change is the first step to being able to navigate wherever you want to go, including visiting Stillness and becoming your life purpose.

Your journey through Be Your Purpose will develop your capacity to strategically direct the flow of Silence, the life moving through your inner world.

MAKE THE COMMITMENT

I encourage you to commit very seriously to the One Small Change. From this moment on, you will listen to your inner dialogue. Create a habit of paying close attention to what is arising in your inner world each moment. Paying close attention is a big part of what actually causes change to your inner dialogue, which in turn will open new routes in the inner world. When you follow Silence as it flows down these paths, you'll be able to experience a dimension of life that you could not access before.

The first step is your commitment to make the One Small Change to your persistent inner dialogue whenever you encounter doubt.

"I'm learning exactly how people who have navigated their inner world to become their purpose did it, and I'm following in their footsteps, step by step."

Are you committed to reminding yourself that you are learning exactly how people who have succeeded in reaching Stillness did it? Are you committed to following in their footsteps, step by step? Can you feel the intention and the expectation of success fill your body—your inner world? Are you prepared to make your journey through your inner world to visit Stillness the priority of your life for a while?

Yes?

Yes!

You've completed Step 1: Making the One Small Change.

You've also committed to making the One Small Change *every time* your persistent inner dialogue arises during the course of your journey:

"I'm learning exactly how people who have navigated their inner world to become their purpose did it, and I'm following in their footsteps step by step."

Congratulations! It's time for Step 2. I'll be with you each step of the way.

STEP 2

Visiting Your Bridge of Translation

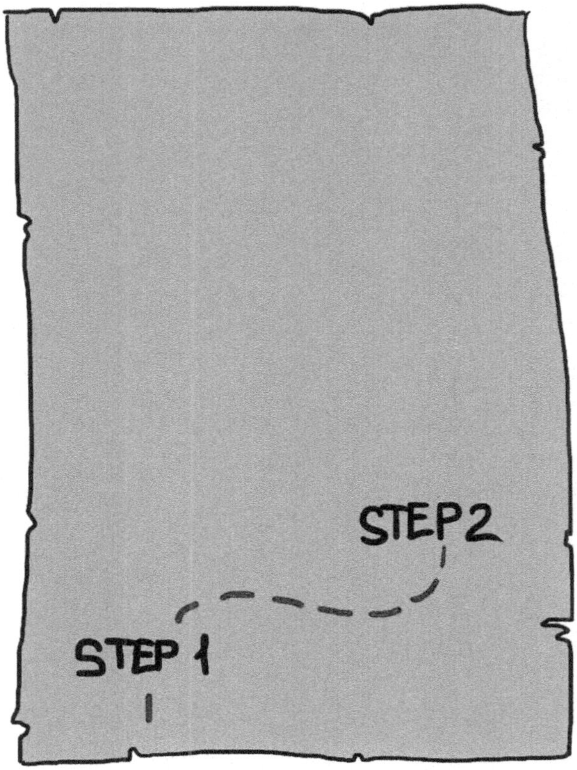

STEP 2: VISITING YOUR BRIDGE OF TRANSLATION

Do not seek to follow in the footsteps of the masters. Seek what they sought.

—Matsuo Basho

Let's go back to that meditation class. I became consciously aware of my inner dialogue for the first time. An inner movie appeared, and I had no idea that I had been creating one until then. In that instant, I learned that my inner movie was constantly broadcasting, whether I wanted it or not. In fact, it was produced whether I even agreed with it or not!

I might never have returned to listen to my inner dialogue that way again if I hadn't been startled out of meditation by the insight. In spite of my resistant thoughts, I knew I had experienced something new, and I realized that my unconscious inner movie was actually creating my emotional experience.

I walked out of that classroom with a flicker of hope: Reality wasn't making me miserable; it was patterns of thinking that I wasn't intending to produce! And yet, it was *seven years* before my first visit to Stillness. It was *another seven years* before I fully understood scientifically how to navigate through my inner dialogue to visit Stillness at will.

Instead of visiting Stillness, I stumbled through more years of heartache. I graduated. I started a company. I struggled. I was not very happy. I was consumed by the memory of the break-up, and it derailed my inner world journey. My path had no structure or consistency.

Through the fog, however, I became aware of a second truth: Not only did my inner dialogue shape my emotional experience, but I had the power to influence my inner dialogue. I started to envision the architecture of my inner world, and I realized that there was a place within it that was the key to understanding how the inner and outer worlds collide and combine: the Bridge of Translation.

You and I will go to the Bridge of Translation together in Step 2.

OBSERVING THE INNER WORLD

The way to navigate your brain and body—your inner world—begins with being able to observe the workings of your brain and body in real time. Throughout *Be Your Purpose*, by learning to observe your inner world in real time and process information in new ways, you will learn to bring more of the content of your inner movie into your conscious awareness.

I've worked with many people who had failed to observe the inner movies. They maintained mistaken stories about who they were, how they function, and what they were capable of achieving. Learning to observe their inner movie in real time allowed them to consistently connect with Silence and become their life's purpose.

But observing your inner world in real time can be a battle. Remember my story? It took me more than a decade to figure out how to listen to and watch my inner world with intensity and consistency. I was susceptible to distracting noise in my brain.

I was under stress, and my stress fed my distraction. Until I discovered the shortcut to accessing my inner dialogue: the Bridge of Translation.

It won't take years for you to journey to Stillness. You'll navigate a far more direct journey than I did because together we will navigate directly to the Bridge of Translation. The power of the Bridge of Translation cannot be overstated.

THE BRIDGE OF TRANSLATION

You may remember the Bridge of Translation from the preparation section, where I introduced it as a landmark of the inner world—one that enables conversation between your inner and outer worlds. When you can journey to the Bridge of Translation, you are at the nexus of your inner world—it is responsible for your inner movie, in fact.

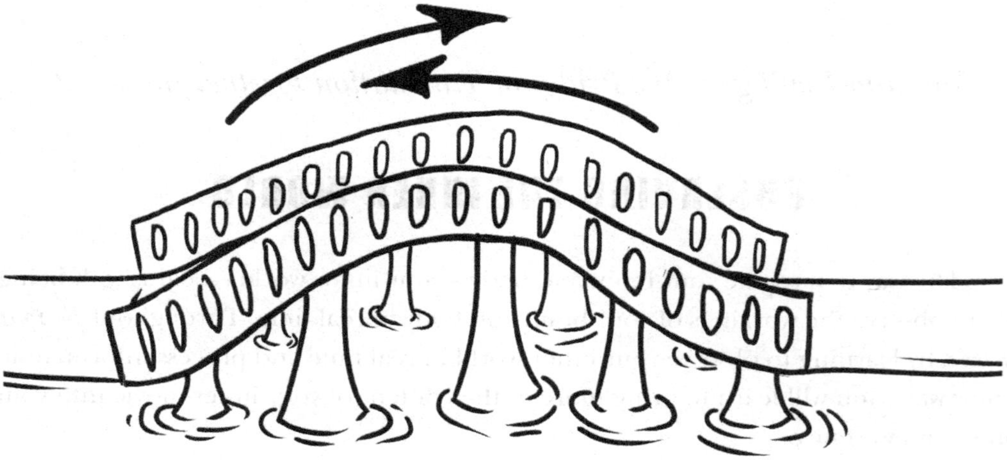

The Bridge of Translation regulates the traffic between the inner and outer worlds.

By reaching the Bridge of Translation, you can immediately access your inner movie. Not only that, but you can use it to influence your inner world journey.

Whether you are aware of it or not, the bridge is constantly working; your inner dialogue flows off of it continually. The ongoing conversation that occurs inside your brain—whether you are consciously thinking about something or you are just listening without effort—is an ever-bubbling translation of the Silence that is flowing through you into your inner dialogue. The Bridge of Translation adjusts the meaning of this incoming information by applying your assumptions, beliefs, and intentions.

From all of this, your Bridge of Translation produces your SELF—each and every moment. Your SELF is your personal experience and expression of life in this moment—your body colliding with your world each moment.

Your SELF is the translation of your inner dialogue each moment.

When you can focus on your SELF as it is created each moment, you are observing the place where all of your life's adventure is processed. This is the place where all your new insights are realized, all your personal inner world cultivation occurs—and where your unique life purpose will be revealed. Observing your inner world is engaging in the most profound journey you could ever make. This is watching the actual journey of your life.

WHY IT WORKS

Brain science research has revealed that your inner world physiology—and so, your experience of your inner world—is completely different when you are stressed versus when you are relaxed. How you experience the outer world is similarly affected by stress. And yet, the incessant thoughts of inner dialogue tend to produce stress in the body.

Until you intentionally bring your inner dialogue into your conscious awareness, your life will reflect the contents, patterns, and habits of conversation that you absorbed as an infant and toddler. You unknowingly define your life using others' interests, prejudices, and conceptions. These pull you from your awareness of Silence—your path of purpose.

Through Mind Exercise (which is a form of meditation), you will connect to Silence and begin to see your inner world with increasingly clarity. At the Bridge of Translation, you have immediate access to the way your inner world and outer world collide. You'll see how stress is produced and when stress is reduced. You'll learn to see your inner world with increasing clarity. Soon, you'll have a clear map, which will vastly improve your ability to identify and navigate through potentially distracting inner dialogue.

With practice, you'll experience your life with a quieted mind. You'll find that one of the most valuable things you can do is slow down, stop, and think only when you choose. This positions you to follow Silence toward Stillness. It allows you to enjoy a qualitatively different life experience.

EXPECT YOURSELF TO CHANGE

By observing and shifting inner dialogue, you'll learn how to move your emotional state back into awareness of Silence on demand. You will move ever closer to the deepest pool of wisdom there is: Stillness. When you eventually remove thoughts from your inner experience, even for a short time, a very real shift occurs in your inner world. This will change your life forever.

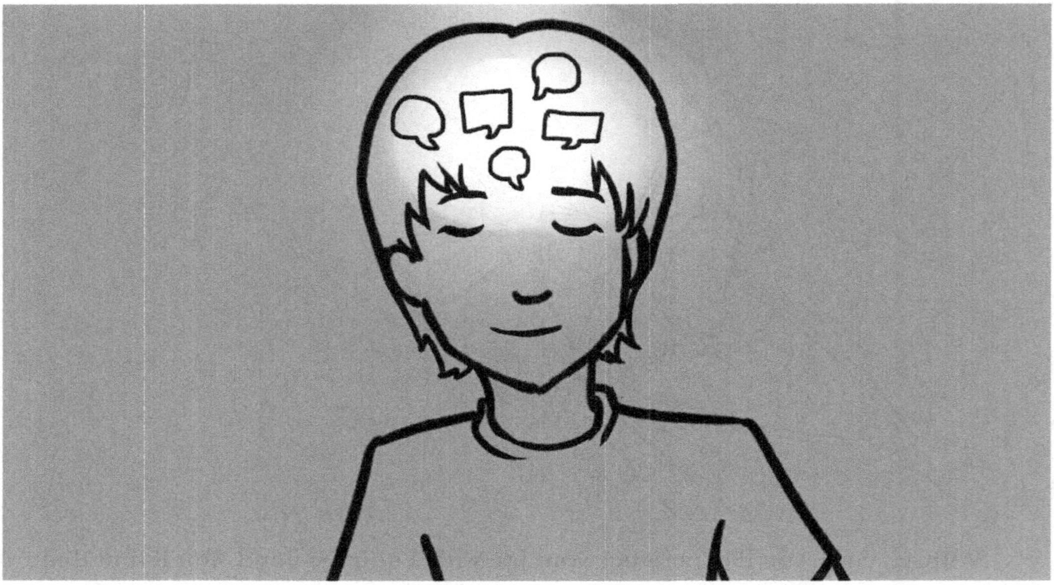

You will learn to take control of your inner conversation, and your life will change.

Today, I look back on the day my college girlfriend broke my heart, and I see the catalyst for the most positive growth in my life. It felt like the worst pain, and I wasn't sure I could recover. Instead, it led me to develop the inner world awareness to be my purpose. I look back with deep gratitude at that moment.

If you are struggling with heartache, loss, doubt, or other emotional pain, know that your worst days can be turned into the most important transitional days of your life too. Keep following the steps through your inner world, and you'll arrive in Stillness.

Remember, whenever you encounter doubt along the way, remind yourself:

"I'm learning exactly how people who have navigated their inner world to become their purpose did it, and I'm following in their footsteps step by step."

You're ready. It's time to visit your Bridge of Translation together, where you can observe the workings of your brain and body in real time. You'll begin listening to your ongoing stream of automatic thoughts—your bubbling inner dialogue, as it arises and flows off the Bridge of Translation. It's time for your first Mind Exercise.

Ready?

Let's go.

You may access a video version of the Step 2 Mind Exercise that follows at BeYourPurpose.com.

MIND EXERCISE

Visiting Your Bridge of Translation

Welcome to your STEP 2 Mind Exercise!

Experience the silent life flowing through your body—Silence.

Welcome to your first Mind Exercise! Don't be intimidated. Remember, these are simply directed meditations that improve your inner strength and function. Just like with physical exercise, the first few times may feel unfamiliar. Keep practicing, and your comfort and ease will grow.

Since it's your first Mind Exercise, I'll start with a tiny bit of background. Your Step 2 Mind Exercise actually is the foundation for the Daily Ritual. (It's recreated in Appendix A and available in video form on *BeYourPurpose.com*, so don't worry about committing the page number or the exercise to memory.) Whenever you need to reconnect with Silence, the Daily Ritual is a great place to start—so think of this Mind Exercise as your launching point for the amazing adventure that is visiting Stillness. It's a place you will return to again and again.

I have one more key piece of advice for you: In general, start your Mind Exercise and Daily Ritual with five minutes of physical exercise—anything you choose, as long as it gets your heart rate up. (For now, and even in Step 3, you might choose to skip the exercise, but prioritize it as part of the process after that.) There are many reasons and benefits to this, which I detail in Appendix B, but the short version is simply this: Physical exercise primes you to get the most out of your Mind Exercise.

If you'd like to exercise now, go ahead. If not, that's okay too. Either way, you're embarking on an exciting journey.

When you're ready, let's begin...

Begin your Mind Exercise sitting comfortably and focusing all of your attention on sensing the tingling occurring in your body right now. I want you to focus on simply feeling how alive your body is.

Take a moment to consider exactly what I'm asking you to do. You possess the ability to place your conscious attention directly into any specific location in your body that you choose, and you can sense the precise sensations, tingling, heat, energy—a translation of the silent energy of life that we call Silence—flowing into that specific location of your body this very moment.

Placing your attention into a part of your body to notice how it feels is such a routine task that you usually take this ability for granted. Right now, though, I want you to honor this superpower for the miraculous gift that it is. Throughout your journey, you are going to intentionally and strategically develop your capacity to access this inner world navigation tool.

As you improve your ability to place your conscious attention into your inner world to sense and connect to the Silence flowing through you, you'll notice that your entire body actually buzzes or tingles. Placing your complete attention into your body connects you to an incredible feeling of aliveness. This is the energy of Silence flowing through you.

You can feel Silence flowing into and through you.

Right now, softly press the heel of your right foot down on the big toe of your left foot, then release the pressure on your left big toe. Focus all your attention on sensing the tingling that occurs as the blood rushes in. Feel it?

Spend a few seconds noticing the tingling, then move your attention around your body. Recognize the tingling that is always occurring in your body—usually without your awareness. Shift your attention to the tingling in the other parts of your left foot. After a bit, notice how the tingling feels in your ankle, then in your calf.

Slowly move your attention up your leg and around your body as you choose, always focusing on the tingling sensation. If you get distracted during this task, just acknowledge what distracted you and then return your attention to where you left off.

Don't judge yourself for losing attention. Each time you notice that you became distracted and return your focus to your body, you are training your attention and your brain to perform at its best—you are taking a small step toward your intended destination: Stillness.

Close your eyes now and notice the subtle tingling in different areas of your body for two minutes.

Ready to notice your body's genius for two minutes?

Go.

Done with two minutes?

Good job. Let's keep Mind Exercising.

Now, listen to each sound you hear, especially sounds that normally go unnoticed. Allow your attention to move around the outer world—the world that exists outside your brain and body. Perhaps your attention will bounce from listening to a car moving toward and then driving away, or maybe you'll hear birds chirping. I want you to notice any sound that usually hums along without notice.

Without agenda, simply listen by placing your conscious attention into a state of open receptivity to the outer world. By directing your brain and body to focus outside yourself, in the outer world, you exercise your superpower of sensing the changes in vibration that are occurring each moment in the world that surrounds you.

When you listen intensely, you may begin to hear the world's pulse beneath the vibrating sound that arises—this pulse is Silence flowing through the outer world, all around you.

As before, if your attention has wandered, take note of what distracted you and then return your attention to listening. Again, don't judge yourself. Every return to attention is a small step toward your destination—you are training your brain and body to navigate your journey to Stillness.

Ready to close your eyes and listen for two minutes?

Go.

Two minutes

Done with two minutes?

Good job. Let's keep Mind Exercising.

So far you've shifted your attention from your inner world to the outer world. Now I want you to shift your attention solely to the air that comes into your body and leaves your body. Notice as it brushes against your nostrils and fills your lungs. Place your full attention into your breath—a conduit between your inner world and the outer world.

As you observe, allow your breath to grow deeper, bringing your attention to the calm depths of the ocean beneath your Bridge of Translation. Breathe in and out comfortably, with all of your attention on the flowing air that sustains your life, allowing your breath its natural desire to grow deeper and slower with each breath—in and out.

As before, if you notice your attention has wandered anytime, just acknowledge what distracted you, what thought arose in your inner world. Return your attention to noticing your breath, and don't judge yourself. Again, each time you return your attention, you are navigating your journey to Stillness.

Ready to close your eyes and notice only your breath for two minutes?

Go.

Done with two minutes?

Good job. Let's keep Mind Exercising.

In the last minutes, you shifted your attention from your outer world—the world that exists outside your brain and body—to your breath, a conduit between your outer world and your inner world.

Continue now by shifting your attention to observing ideas arising in your inner world—your thoughts. I want you to move your attention toward where these thoughts emerge. This is your Bridge of Translation, where you can observe how the silent life energy that flows through you—Silence—is translated into the ongoing conversation that takes place inside your head. Follow these steps to find your own bridge and begin to build a map of your inner world.

First, be open to the sense of emerging thought. Orient your attention on the space within you into which they arise. Second, shift your attention to observing the emerging thoughts. You may have to wait patiently for a thought to appear. When it arrives, know you have discovered the location of your Bridge of Translation. Third, create a mental image of the Bridge of Translation on your own inner world map.

I want you to actually see your Bridge of Translation in your inner world. Visualize its location, and see your thoughts and ideas flowing off of it.

Listen to and watch the translation of Silence into your thoughts and your SELF, flowing off your bridge. Notice the first thought arise and fade away. Then, notice the next thought that arises and fades away.

If you notice that your attention wandered during this task, perhaps being carried away into a stream of your thoughts—a developing inner movie—just direct your attention back to observing the thoughts flowing off your Bridge of Translation. Again, don't judge yourself. Each time, you are training your brain and body to navigate your journey to Stillness. You are taking a small step toward your destination.

Ready to close your eyes and visit your Bridge of Translation and listen for two minutes?

Go.

Done with two minutes?

Great work!

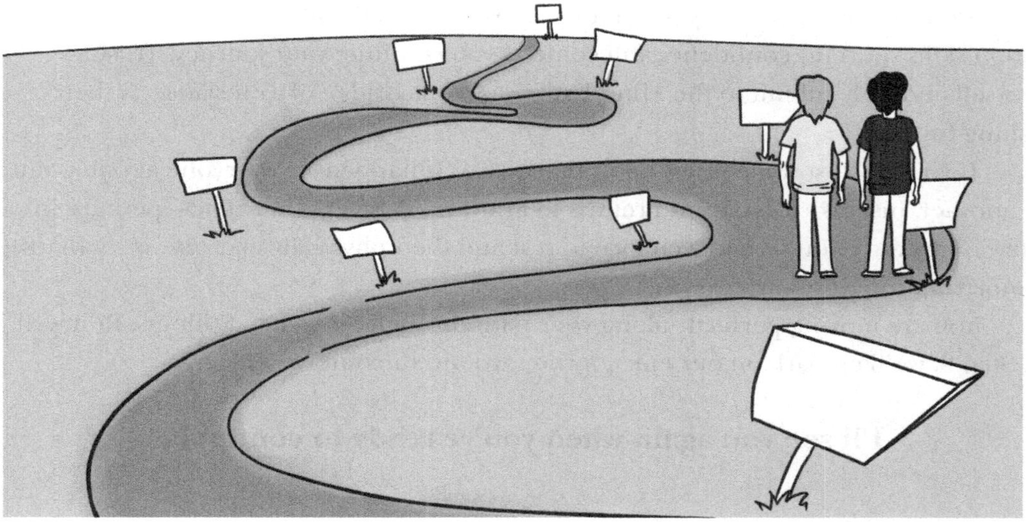

You've completed Step 2.

Did that last sentence worry you? You're not alone. After completing Step 2, many readers wonder whether they completed the Mind Exercise correctly. Most likely your mind wandered for a bit here and there. This is completely normal. Everyone experiences a wandering mind during Mind Exercises. Everyone also intermittently forgets the task of Mind Exercise they intended to focus on.

Distracted attention does not mean you are Mind Exercising incorrectly. Each time you bring your attention back to the Mind Exercise task at hand you are Mind Exercising perfectly in that moment. Intentionally and strategically reorienting your attention is the journey that will take you to Stillness.

I've also had clients tell me they aren't sure that they found their "real" Bridge of Translation. I believe this is actually your One Thought rearing its ugly head again. Respond with the One Small Change:

"I'm learning exactly how people who have navigated their inner world to become their purpose did it, and I'm following in their footsteps step by step."

Your map is a good map, even if you haven't gained confidence in your navigation skills yet. This confidence will come as you continue your journey. Trust in yourself and fully submit to the Mind Exercises. Your Bridge of Translation is there, waiting for you.

If you feel lost sometimes, know that's okay. It happens to everyone at one point or another. Just take a break and return to Mind Exercise another time—perhaps in a few hours after you've had a chance to rest and then physically exercise, or perhaps tomorrow or in a couple days.

You are moving perfectly along your path through Silence to Stillness. Rest well. In Step 3, we'll embark on our epic journey around the outer world.

I'll see you again when you're ready to continue.

STEP 3

Identifying Resistance to Being Your Purpose

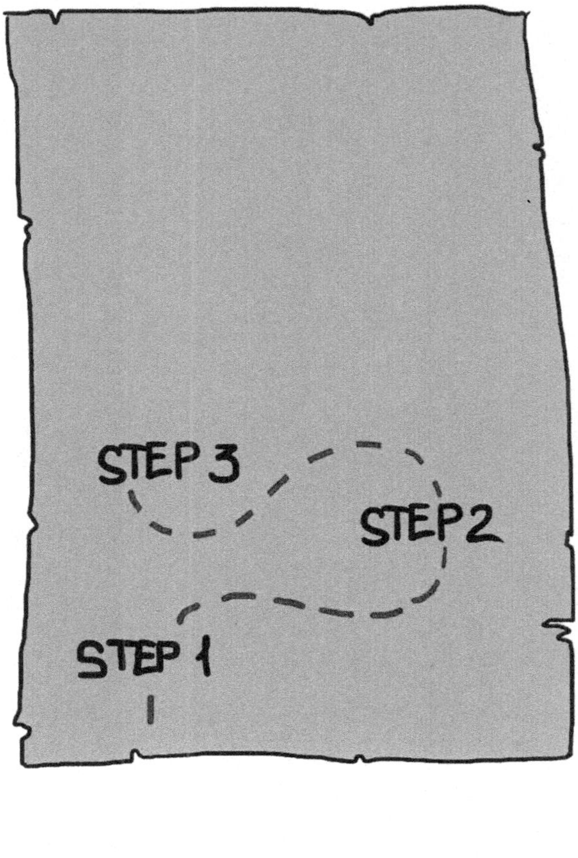

STEP 3: IDENTIFYING RESISTANCE TO BEING YOUR PURPOSE

A path is always longer the first time we traverse it.

—Thomas Mann

Once I found my Bridge of Translation, I gained newfound confidence in my ability to connect to Silence. I was fascinated by the brain science behind it, and I earned my doctorate in clinical psychology while simultaneously prioritizing my connection to Silence.

In so many ways, it was a really positive time for me. I was learning and growing by leaps and bounds both personally and professionally. I built a practice, and a home, in San Francisco. I spent most of my free time listening to Silence in the peace of nature, making notes about how psychology and brain science related to visiting Stillness.

As I listened, I began to feel a new call of life purpose bubbling within. Whenever I connected to Silence deeply, I heard a call to journey around the world—the outer world—and write about how I navigate my inner world to visit Stillness. Ideas about where to go, what I could learn, and how I could share my experiences began flowing onto my bridge more insistently.

To my surprise, as I heard my "new" purpose flowing through Silence more clearly, I also began hearing one challenge after another discouraging me from embracing it. How could I leave behind my patients, many of whom were making great strides and with whom I felt such a rapport? What about my friends and family? How was I going to pay for this, especially without an agent or publisher signed on? What about that amazing woman I just started dating—did I really want to push our relationship to the backburner after so many years of being alone?

Making an extended international trip seemed like a major financial, professional, and personal risk. My inner dialogue noise increased; my inner peace and my connection to Silence were increasingly compromised.

Fear of being my purpose began to arise in my inner world.

My purpose was invariably being countered by a specific, arising version of SELF who disconnected me from Silence and convinced me to delay. After months of wrestling with this, I began to see the fearful version of my SELF with more clarity during my Mind Exercise. As I watched, and consistently returned my attention to my bridge each time distraction arose, an inner movie emerged: A scared little boy sat at the edge of the pool. Slowly, uncertainly, he dipped one foot in. And then he froze—unwilling or unable to move.

The scared boy arose each time I contemplated the next step on my evolving path.

I clearly saw this movie, over and over, but it took a long time to acknowledge this boy's fear as my own. Only then was I able to realize that unless I valued being my purpose more than I feared its potential consequences, the small boy would continue to freeze; my inner dialogue would continue to produce reasons to delay.

In time, I decided to confront my fear. I took a concrete step on my new path. I moved from San Francisco to a cottage in Calistoga, California, to prioritize writing *Be Your Purpose.* With that unequivocal commitment to Silence and real, honest action toward it, the path to my purpose prevailed over the fearful version of my SELF.

For one hundred days, I quieted my inner world with Mind Exercise and laid the groundwork for my epic journey around the world. I sold my car and bought a one-way ticket. The epic journey began—but only because I was able to identify my fearful SELF, confront it, and take action.

RESISTANCE

In today's Mind Exercise you'll directly confront the idea of living out your life's highest purpose. When you do, you'll observe your own automatically arising patterns of thought, emotion—perhaps an inner movie. You've already seen how your inner dialogue bubbles to the surface of the waters of your brain, flowing onto the Bridge of Translation. Now, you'll see there's even more to it.

Just as I uncovered how and why I was automatically resisting my outer world journey, you'll uncover inner impulses to take action or perhaps to remain frozen still. You'll begin to observe your instincts and emotions arising in real time into scenes playing out in your inner world.

In those moments, you'll be able to identify your own fearful SELF—or, perhaps in your case, your SELF may be reluctant, cynical, disbelieving, or even angry. This is your resistance: the automatic reaction that interferes with taking the next step toward the life you are supposed to live.

Resistance is any reaction that distracts you from moving toward and becoming your life purpose.

Keep in mind that resistance comes in too many forms to list. You might even hear yourself saying, *But I don't even know what my life purpose is! How can I take any steps toward it?* That's resistance—it's a reaction that blocks you from moving forward. (And remember: Being your purpose doesn't mean you have a higher calling to something specific; it means you can listen to your inner world well enough to hear the next step in your life. It means you can listen without being distracted away from listening because of fear. It means you are fulfilled by the life you live.)

Resistance will arise in your inner world. It happens to everyone. Whatever resistance arises, just take note. In future steps, we will work together on advanced strategies to navigate around these distractions as you progress to Stillness.

PRACTICE MAKES PERFECT(ISH)

Remember, visiting Stillness requires remaining connected to Silence regardless of how it morphs as it flows through your inner world each moment. The better you get at identifying the range of experiences and distractions—in other words, your resistances—the more equipped you'll be to remain connected consistently.

Through practice, you can learn to maintain a connection to Silence in the face of a variety of distractions.

There's only one surefire way to develop the inner world mastery necessary to visit Stillness strategically, though: daily practice.

Inner world distractions tend to arise in repetitive patterns. Implementing daily inner world practice habits is the best way to identify these patterns. You'll develop essential knowledge about your inner world patterns and expand your awareness of how your inner world functions. And here's the best part: Once you identify them, you can change them.

In your Daily Ritual and the subsequent Mind Exercises, you'll practice noticing thoughts and other bodily experiences that are strong enough to surface on the waters of your mind and emerge onto your Bridge of Translation. You'll become an expert at identifying the sensations and emotions that represent the impulses that arise in your inner world. This expertise is a vital aspect in learning to direct your attention strategically in your inner world.

WHY IT WORKS

As noted above, unconscious resistance arises in everyone. Although we each aspire to a life of purpose, unconscious fears arise in the face of that. We often unconsciously resist listening to Silence. Until you identify precisely how and when fears related to hearing and living out your purpose arise in you, automatic inner world reactions can prevent you from progressing along your path to Stillness.

Unconscious resistance prevents most people from discovering and ever becoming their purpose.

For decades, brain scientists have known about "automatic thoughts" in one's inner world. Dr. Aaron Beck at the University of Pennsylvania pioneered this research, resulting in his cognitive theory and related cognitive therapy. In fact, cognitive theory is the foundation for the most common clinical practices today.

It's based on a very simple idea: People have automatic thoughts—streams of thought that arise without prompting (in other words, your inner dialogue). Often, these inner world thoughts are negative, which in turn influence emotions and outer world reactions in a negative way. That's the brain-body connection in action.

But if you learn to identify these automatic thoughts, you can also learn to change them. More than fifty years of brain science research have taught us that anyone can make personal changes to their inner dialogue, once they identify it. In other words, if you can name your resistance—the fearful SELF—you can remain connected to Silence even as your fearful SELF attempts to distract you from it. The constant connection then allows you make changes you want to make to progress toward Stillness.

You've already seen the power of this research in action, by making the One Small Change and bringing your inner dialogue into your conscious awareness. By repeating these actions, your brain will actually change in response. Your brain will change even more drastically as you master the connection to Silence in the face of distraction. Every day that you practice these inner world techniques, your physical body adapts incrementally too.

BEGIN THE DAILY RITUAL

With that in mind, it's important to be consistent in your practice. That's why I've created the Daily Ritual—a sequence of Mind Exercises that refines your connection to Silence. You've already successfully completed part of the Daily Ritual in the Step 2 Mind Exercise. Today, I will walk you through the full Daily Ritual for the first time.

Repetition is an intentional aspect of every Mind Exercise, including the Daily Ritual.

Repetition is essential when you are learning to observe your inner world effectively, which is why you should complete the Daily Ritual every day from now until you finish your journey to Stillness.

During the Daily Ritual and Mind Exercises, you may encounter strong impulses like hunger or restlessness journeying through your inner world to the surface of the waters of your mind. They then emerge onto your Bridge of Translation. Simply sense or "listen" to each one; observe its influence on your inner world. (For example, if you sense an itch, don't scratch. Just become aware of the sensation.) As you learn to do this consistently, you'll deeply connect to Silence.

Again, five minutes (or more) of physical exercise will become a key component to the Daily Ritual. This primes your body to connect to Silence and stimulates brain cell growth. For today, you can choose to start simply by reminding yourself:

"I'm learning exactly how people who have navigated their inner world to become their purpose did it, and I'm following in their footsteps step by step."

That's it. That's all it takes to prepare your physical body for your inner world journey.

Once you complete the Daily Ritual, your Step 3 Mind Exercise focuses your attention on inner world activity, allowing you to observe what occurs inside you when you confront the challenge of committing to being your purpose.

Ready for your Step 3 Mind Exercise?

Let's go.

You may access a video version of the Step 3 Mind Exercise that follows at BeYourPurpose.com.

MIND EXERCISE

THE DAILY RITUAL AND IDENTIFYING RESISTANCE

WELCOME TO YOUR STEP 3 MIND EXERCISE!

Identify the resistance that is blocking you from being your purpose.

Let's start with the Daily Ritual.

Just as you did in Step 2, begin your Mind Exercise sitting comfortably and focusing all of your attention on sensing the tingling occurring in your body right now. I want you to focus on simply feeling how alive your body is.

When you notice the tingling of your body, you experience the flow of Silence through you.

Again, just as in Step 2, softly press the heel of your right foot down on the big toe of your left foot, then release the pressure on your left big toe. Focus all your attention on sensing the tingling that occurs as the blood rushes in. Feel it?

After you've felt the tingling for a few seconds, begin to move your attention to notice the tingling in different areas of your body. For example, shift your attention to the tingling in the other parts of your left foot. After a bit, notice how the tingling feels in your ankle, then in your calf.

Slowly move your attention up your leg and around your body as you choose, always focusing on the tingling sensation. If you get distracted during this task, just acknowledge what distracted you and then return your attention to where you left off.

Don't judge yourself for losing attention. Each time you notice that you became distracted and return your focus to your body, you are training your attention and your brain to perform at its best—you are taking a small step toward your intended destination: Stillness.

Ready to close your eyes and feel your body's bubbling genius—the subtle tingling in different areas of your body—for two minutes?

Go.

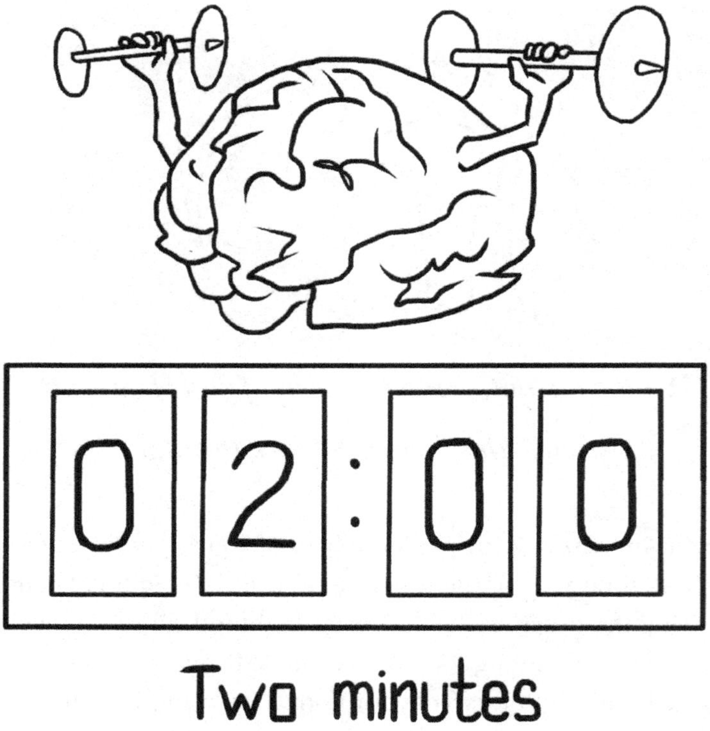

Done with two minutes?

Good job. Let's keep Mind Exercising.

Now, listen to each sound you hear, especially sounds that normally go unnoticed. Allow your attention to move around the outer world—the world that exists outside your brain and body. Perhaps your attention will bounce from listening to a car moving toward and then driving away, or maybe you'll hear birds chirping. I want you to notice any sound that usually hums along without notice.

Without agenda, simply listen by placing your conscious attention into a state of open receptivity to whatever sounds arise in the outer world. When you listen intensely, you may begin to hear the world's pulse beneath the vibrating sound that arises—this pulse is Silence flowing through the outer world, all around you.

As before, if your attention has wandered, take note of what distracted you and then return your attention to listening. Don't judge yourself. Every return to attention is a small step toward your destination—you are training your brain and body to navigate your journey to Stillness.

Ready to close your eyes and listen for two minutes?

Go.

Done with two minutes?

Good job. Let's keep Mind Exercising.

So far you've shifted your attention from your inner world to the outer world. Now I want you to shift your attention solely to the air that comes into your body and leaves your body. Notice as it brushes against your nostrils and fills your lungs. Place your full attention into your breath—a conduit between your inner world and the outer world.

As you observe, allow your breath to grow deeper, bringing your attention to the calm depths of the ocean beneath your Bridge of Translation. Breathe in and out comfortably, with all of your attention on the flowing air that sustains your life, allowing your breath its natural desire to grow deeper and slower with each breath—in and out.

If you notice your attention has wandered anytime, just acknowledge what distracted you, what thought arose in your inner world. Return your attention to noticing your breath, and don't judge yourself. Each time you return your attention, you are navigating your journey to Stillness.

Ready to close your eyes and notice only your breath for two minutes?

Go.

Done with two minutes?

Good job. Let's keep Mind Exercising.

In the last minutes, you shifted your attention from your outer world—the world that exists outside your brain and body—to your breath, a conduit between your outer world and your inner world.

Continue now by shifting your attention to observing ideas arising in your inner world—your thoughts. I want you to move your attention toward where these thoughts emerge. This is your Bridge of Translation, where you can observe how the silent life energy that flows through you—Silence—is translated into the ongoing conversation that takes place inside your head. Follow these steps to find your own bridge and continue building a map of your inner world.

First, be open to the sense of emerging thought. Orient your attention on the space within you into which they arise. Second, shift your attention to observing the emerging thoughts. You may have to wait patiently for a thought to appear. When it arrives, know you have discovered the location of your Bridge of Translation. Third, note its location on your own inner world map.

Observe your Bridge of Translation, off of which all your thoughts and ideas flow.

Listen to and watch the translation of Silence into your thoughts and your SELF, flowing off your bridge. Notice the first thought arise and fade away. Then, notice the next thought that arises and fades away.

If you notice that your attention wandered during this task, perhaps being carried away into a stream of your thoughts—a developing inner movie—just direct your attention back to observing the thoughts flowing off your bridge of Translation. Again, don't judge yourself. Each time, you are training your brain and body to navigate your journey to Stillness. You are taking a small step toward your destination.

Ready to close your eyes and visit your Bridge of Translation and listen for two minutes?

Go.

Done with two minutes?

Great work! Let's keep Mind Exercising.

Now I want you to experience your entire body tingling or buzzing. Shift your attention away from your thoughts and into feeling the Silence flowing through your entire body. Just as you noticed tingling in specific areas of your body before, feel Silence flowing now.

Once you connect to Silence, become aware of the precise sensations, instincts, intuitions, or impulses arising in your inner world. For example, you may notice arising impulses such as thirst, hunger, lust, sleepiness, or boredom.

If you sense anything arising through the buzz of Silence, just feel and listen. Observe the influence on your inner world. Do not seek to gratify the impulse. Simply become aware of the sensation for a moment. Then let it go, and reconnect to Silence.

Maybe something you experience is trying to speak to you, like an intuition. Just listen to your inner world. Then let it go as you reconnect to Silence.

Ready to close your eyes and feel Silence flowing through your entire body, to notice sensations, impulses, intuitions, and instincts arising in your inner world for one minute?

Go.

Done with one minute?

Good job.

You have completed the Daily Ritual.

Let's complete your Step 3 Mind Exercise now.

Now, we will observe precisely how your inner world reacts in the moments when you consider living up to your full potential. How do you feel when you think about becoming your purpose? How do your body and SELF react?

Ask yourself the following question:

Can I make a one hundred percent commitment
to fully living up to my purpose?

Keep that question in your mind. For the next minute, observe your inner world precisely. You will clearly sense the response that idea provokes in your inner world.

Ready to close your eyes and observe how your inner world responds for one minute?

Go.

Done with one minute?

Good job.

In the blank space below, write down what you noticed arising in your inner world during the last minute. There are no wrong answers. You are just practicing and observing.

My Inner World Reaction

As an example, this is what my inner world reaction looked like when I first attempted this Mind Exercise:

Sean's Inner World Reaction

I feel fear at the prospect of taking on the responsibility of living out my evolving purpose and up to my full potential. I know I want to, but when I truly confronted it, it was like a heavy burden came down on me. I finally put in words that this is a daunting task at which I can fail. I noticed an emerging SELF pulling my attention away from thinking about making the full commitment. Then, I saw a small boy uncertainly dipping one foot in a pool of water. Suddenly freezing still, he was unwilling or unable to move.

Here's another example—this time one that I've imagined based on what my clients have told me, particularly when they're unsure about what being their purpose might look like.

Example Inner World Reaction

It felt like my brain was on infinite repeat; I just kept hearing the same question. "How can I know if I'm doing the right thing?" My chest tightens when I think about it, even. It almost felt like I was back in a job interview for a job I really wanted but knew I wasn't qualified for. I could almost see myself back at the table, trying to figure out if I had the "right" answers... And I knew I couldn't get the job and move up in life if I didn't have them.

Done writing down your inner world reaction?

Great job!

You've completed STEP 3.

You've expanded your awareness of your inner world, and you've observed your personal reaction to the idea of being your purpose. You'll now notice any resistance to being your purpose far more clearly when it arises in the future. You are continuing to add color, texture, and depth to your map of the inner world, allowing you to strategically journey toward Stillness.

I'll see you again when you're ready to continue.

STEP 4

Observing Your Automatic Responses

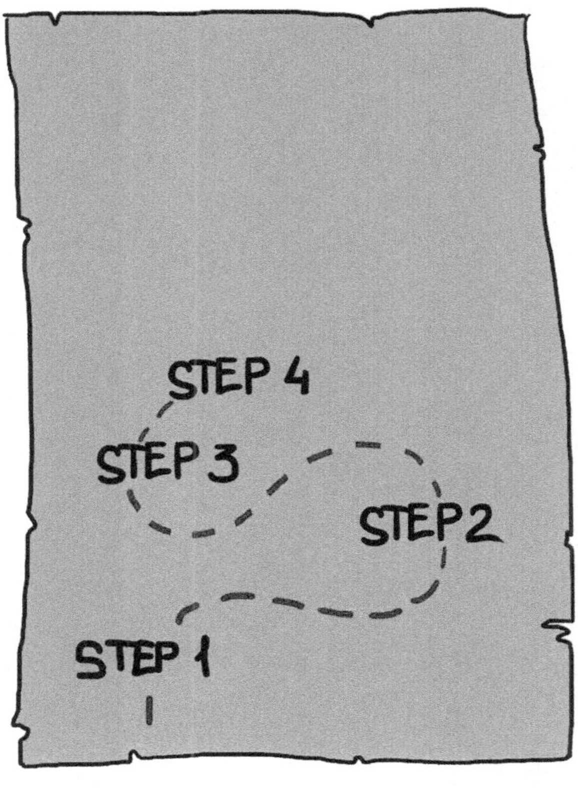

STEP 4: OBSERVING YOUR AUTOMATIC RESPONSES

Being entirely honest with oneself is a good exercise.

—Sigmund Freud

One hundred days listening carefully to my inner dialogue in the Calistoga cottage had prepared me. Being my purpose now meant departing on an epic adventure to visit homes of history's inner world masters, so that's exactly what I did. I followed my call across the Atlantic, navigating my inner world and writing down the steps to visiting Stillness.

I found myself in the hometown of one of the most famous inner world masters of the Western world: Dr. Sigmund Freud. I toured his home office in Vienna, where he analyzed patients for nearly forty years and changed the world with his theories on the influence of past experiences.

I was inspired; my days were filled with researching and writing, enlightened by deep human insights left to us in Dr. Freud's long shadow. Finally, one evening, I put myself in the shoes of one of his patients; I laid down on the psychoanalysis couch myself.

I began to Mind Exercise to quiet my inner world. As Dr. Freud himself would encourage, I pulled up an old memory. Immediately, I felt my body and my emotions shift.

In my mind, I saw myself at my first competitive tennis match. Nine years old, I had been coached by my father, himself a world-class champion. I was sure that I, like my father, was made to be a champion. I arrived with my family in tow and with emotional stakes that couldn't be higher. My confidence was unshakable—until I set foot on the court.

Nothing felt right. Everything—the ball, the fans, the other matches—was moving so fast. My match was an hour-long humiliation. I didn't win a single game, an outcome for which I was singularly unprepared. I shook hands and hurried off the court.

Minutes later, my father found me hiding beside a tree far from the courts. As I watched him approach, my stomach was in knots. "My stomach hurts," I told him, fighting back tears.

"Now?" he asked. I nodded, and he paused. Eventually, he spoke again: "Are you going to be a good player or a great player one day?"

I took two deep breaths. "A great player?" I responded tentatively.

"Yes, a great player," he said. He waited another minute or so. "How does your stomach feel now?"

I was surprised by the question, but I was even more surprised to discover that my pain was swiftly disappearing. The difference was stark. "Better!"

"Good. Time to practice. Let's go when you're ready," my hero said as he stood up.

As I replayed the story in my inner world, I could feel my body respond to the emotions of me as a nine-year-old. And I grasped something I couldn't at the tennis match: My thoughts created the story in my head, which in turn changed my emotional and physical state. That was my first experience with the true power of inner dialogue.

As I laid on the couch in deference to Freud's memory, I startled from the image with gratitude. Not because of the pain, but because, thankfully, my pain was cultivated into a lesson that day. My father took the opportunity to plant a seed of wisdom in me that would flower over the years into a key lesson I now use every day of my life.

THE PAST IN EVERY DAY OF YOUR LIFE

What an impact from one simple exchange. At age nine, I probably thought it was the least important part of the day—paling in comparison to the horrific defeat I'd suffered on the court. And yet, it is in the fabric of my daily life and a foundation of my adult SELF.

This is the inner world mastery pioneered by Dr. Freud: Our behaviors are driven by all sorts of things that occurred in our pasts and that we are not at all conscious of in the present. Every day, however, we act in response to what happened long ago, often automatically. We are reacting to what Dr. Freud called *formative experiences.* This culture-rattling insight changed the course of history, foremost because it changed the way we understand how our SELF develops.

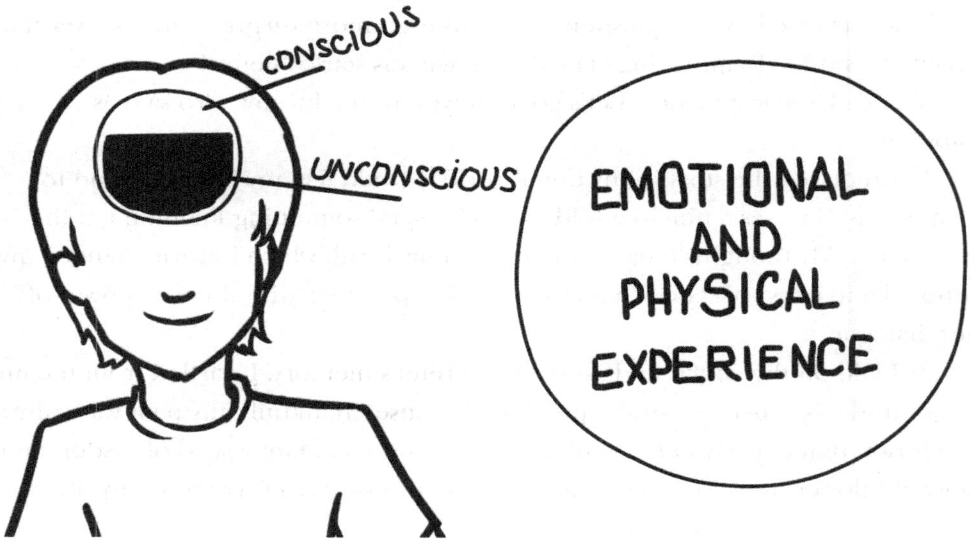

Painful past experiences and fears continue to live within each of us, regardless of our awareness. Although we may have forgotten them—or, indeed, if they occurred before we were even able to form lasting conscious memories—these events continue to inform the moment-to-moment recreation of our SELFs and, so, how we feel and express ourselves today.

In simpler terms, we hold onto challenging or traumatic moments internally. These moments morph into emotions and behaviors later in life. Your current SELF is expressing the original experience *and* the way you interpreted the original experience throughout your life.

Think of these moments like seaweed in the water of your inner world. As the water flows toward the Bridge of Translation, seaweed may cling to its pilings. In some cases, the seaweed can grow and grow—and as it does, it can camouflage and distort the words and images flowing off your bridge. What emerges (in other words, your SELF) is shaped by that seaweed, that clinging past experience.

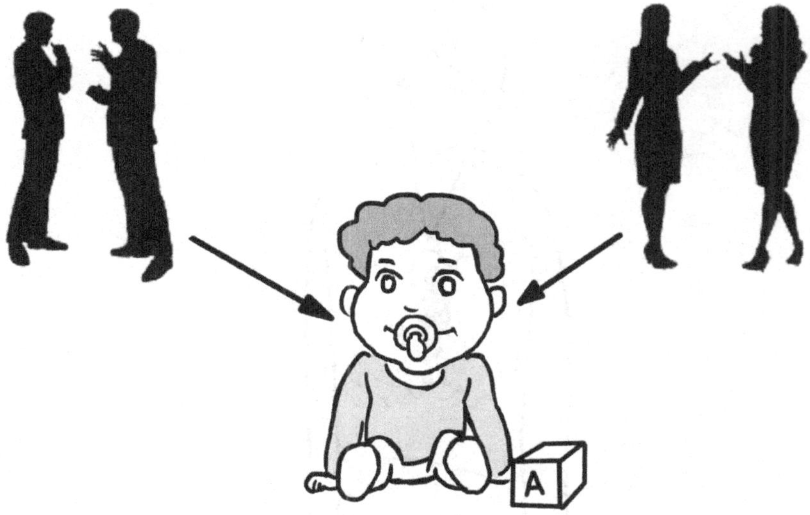

Your history forms the iterations of your SELF that rise off your Bridge of Translation today.

A PROVOCATIVE IMAGE

Observing your inner dialogue intensely allows you to see the ripple effects from the clinging seaweed of past experiences clearly. Until you recognize these ripples, you cannot address them. They will continue to morph into your everyday SELF, perhaps even impeding the flow of Silence.

So in today's Mind Exercise, you will learn to notice these ripples and the automatic emotional habits they morph into. Without awareness, these old patterns of emotion disconnect you from the Silence flowing through you; they derail your journey to Stillness. But with awareness, you can recognize them before they distract you from focusing your attention where you choose.

This is something you can learn, and we'll do it in this Mind Exercise using what I call a *provocative image*. This is any image that provokes emotion in you. My clients usually find that a photo of someone they once loved and who subsequently left their lives is most successful. If you don't have that kind of picture handy, any personally emotionally provocative image will work.

Try not to look at the image just yet. Just set it near you. It will be an aspect of the Step 4 Mind Exercise. In the exercise, you will experience how this outer world image provokes changes in your inner world. In real time, you'll observe how past experiences affect your Bridge of Translation and thus impact how your body feels now. You'll see how Silence is transformed as it flows through your inner world in the midst of particular thoughts or experiences.

WHY IT WORKS

Learning to watch the content arising in the inner world is a core aspect of almost all psychology practice theories in use today. In fact, Dr. Freud is among the many inner world masters who, over thousands of years, developed a variety of meditation practices to enable this sort of observation with remarkable clarity.

In Dr. Freud's case, he developed a therapeutic technique called *free association*, wherein a patient voices his stream of consciousness—i.e., his arising inner dialogue. Listening closely, Dr. Freud excavated the historical roots of his patient's emotional symptoms and/or complaints.

But it's not necessary to have a therapist present, or even to speak aloud. Anyone can learn to connect to Silence and observe their inner world closely. By doing so, you'll develop the ability to notice, and eventually make use of, the history in your life that is stored in your inner world. This becomes your range of SELFs in each moment—the arising contents of your inner dialogue, reproduced and interpreted by your Bridge of Translation.

SELF is just another way of referring to the way your brain and body organize your history of experience in the face of outer world information.

Another way of looking at SELF is as the vast, efficient organization scheme that your brain and body have developed to reliably reproduce your history of experience. Every moment, your inner world is flooded with information that must be filtered and processed through Silence. Without a repetitive way to filter and process, your inner world would not be able to create a consistent inner world experience—an experience of your SELF. The creation of SELF from this processing (via the Bridge of Translation), particularly in the face of constant influx, provides you with a sense of identity, individuality, and personal agency.

When you can observe the content arising in your inner dialogue, you can recognize the repetitive patterns of content that tend to distract your attention. Even more important, you'll learn how to strategically redirect the stories running on automatic repeat. Instead of letting your inner movies and persistent inner dialogue disconnect you from Silence and recreate old emotional habits, you will use strategic emotional visualizations to cultivate the inner world experiences you choose.

Once you experience how your inner world operates, you only need to practice correctly and consistently to fine-tune your mastery.

GIVE YOURSELF SPACE

We know now that listening to your inner dialogue builds awareness of the story your SELF is telling in each moment. However, you need inner world "space" in order to do that with clarity. If you don't maintain adequate space, the story your SELF is telling can overwhelm your connection to Silence. You'll no longer be following its flow toward Stillness; instead, you'll be caught up in the unnecessary emotional turmoil a SELF's story often produces.

We are particularly prone to this because the human brain's repetitive processing pattern is resistant to change. Without intentional intervention, your SELF will keep repeating its most persistent, unconsciously derived stories—like your persistent inner dialogue. When you develop enough inner space to observe your SELF in real time, however, you'll see old patterns turn into automatic emotional habits—perhaps producing wounded, distracting, or unwanted versions of your SELF.

Think of an endless clear sky stretching above and around and endlessly away from your Bridge of Translation. This is the inner world "space" that you can make use of. Think of a bird flying overhead and the view it has of the bridge. It can see and hear the whole bridge, including the ever-changing activity of the flow off of it. Now think of a bird that rests on the railings of the bridge. It can only see what is right in front of it. When something rushes off of the bridge, the bird may get caught up in it.

You want to observe your bridge from the space of the clear sky, like the bird flying overhead. With distance, you can observe the whole picture clearly. When you get too close to your bridge, like the bird who rests on the railings, however, the space around your bridge fades from your awareness. Rather than observing activity, you merge into and become the activity—you become the SELF arising off your bridge.

Each step you take through Be Your Purpose is developing your capacity to observe and direct the SELF that is recreated in your inner world so that you can follow Silence to discover and become your unique purpose.

Ready to observe emotions in your inner world?

Let's go.

THE DAILY RITUAL

Begin today's Mind Exercise by completing the Daily Ritual (starting with five minutes of physical exercise) located in Appendix A. When you have completed the Daily Ritual, return here to complete your Step 4 Mind Exercise. *You may access a video version of the Daily Ritual and Step 4 Mind Exercise at BeYourPurpose.com.*

Done with the Daily Ritual and ready to continue with your Step 4 Mind Exercise?

Good work. Let's keep going.

MIND EXERCISE

Observing Your Automatic Responses

WELCOME TO YOUR STEP 4 MIND EXERCISE!

Learn to observe the automatic emotional habits that distract you from connecting to Silence and being your unique purpose.

In the preparation for this step, you selected a provocative image—a picture that calls up emotions that you cannot resist. Put this image beside you, within reach. Sit quietly with the image turned away.

Do you have your image?

Good.

Observe how you feel in this moment. Maybe you simply feel neutral, or maybe you're happy or bored or anxious. Just make mental notes to yourself about your state of emotion and any thoughts flowing off your bridge. Then, allow yourself to feel calm. Release any inner world activity for now.

Once you feel emotionally neutral for a minute or so, you'll be ready to turn your provocative image toward you. When you're ready to do so, you must truly look at it. As you do, pay attention to how your emotions change in the instant you view the image.

Ready to turn your image toward you?

Go.

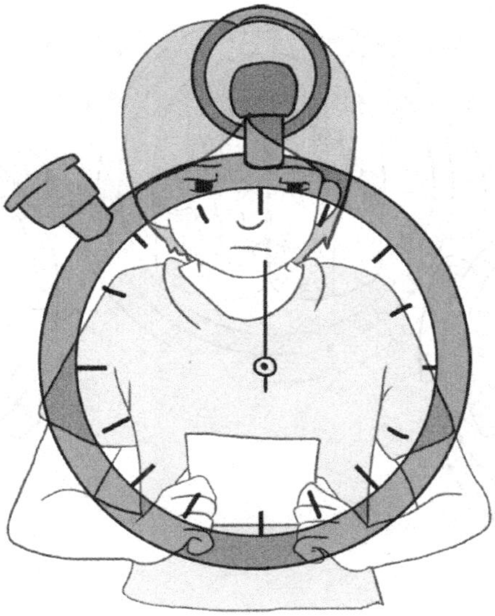

What change do you notice in your inner world?

First, let's think about the process that just happened.... Did you notice that your reaction was automatic—entirely out of your conscious control? Did you notice how such a small change in your environment instantly changed your emotional state? Can you imagine how different your decisions might be when a provocative image influences you?

And now, let's think about your personal reactions.... What feelings emerged from simply looking at a picture? What change did you notice in your inner world? What instincts, thoughts, and beliefs—some of which you may not have even been conscious of before this moment—collided into one another when you saw that provocative image from the outer world?

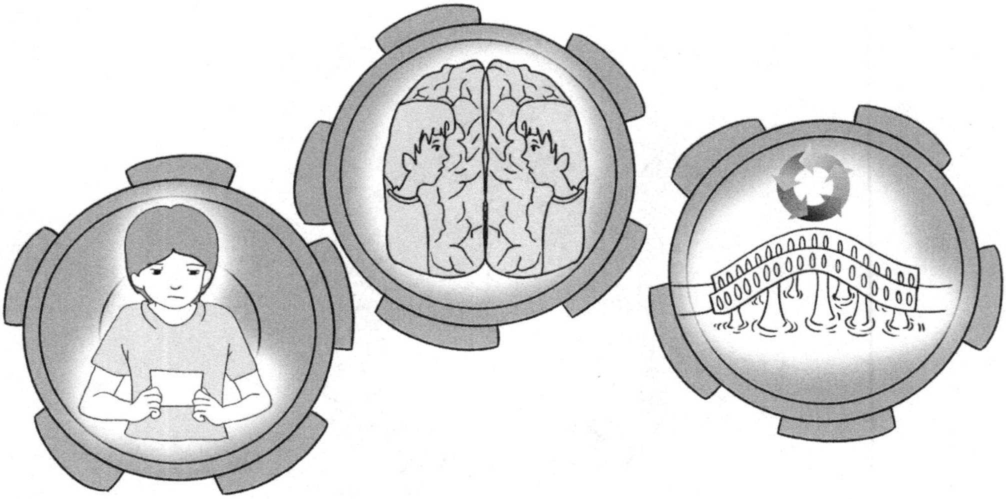

What automatic patterns have been programmed to go on instant repeat in your own inner movies?

If just looking at a simple photo can have such an obvious impact—instantly forcing beliefs, thoughts, instincts, and physical reactions into inner world action that produces immediate emotion (and perhaps behavior)—what are the implications for how your emotional life unfolds in general? And what does this say about the importance of noticing these patterns as they arise in your inner world?

Take a minute now to write down the immediate inner world reaction you noticed as you looked at your provocative image.

My Inner World Reaction

You've completed Step 4.
Congratulations!

By watching an outer world event change your thoughts and emotions, you've further expanded your direct awareness of the range and contents arising in your inner world. In upcoming Mind Exercises, you'll master the skill of noticing unconscious cycles of thought, belief, emotion, and behavior. You'll build your capacity to notice each pattern as it arises, and you'll learn to shift inner world activity whenever you choose.

I'll see you again when you're ready to continue.

STEP 5

Making the Epic Shift

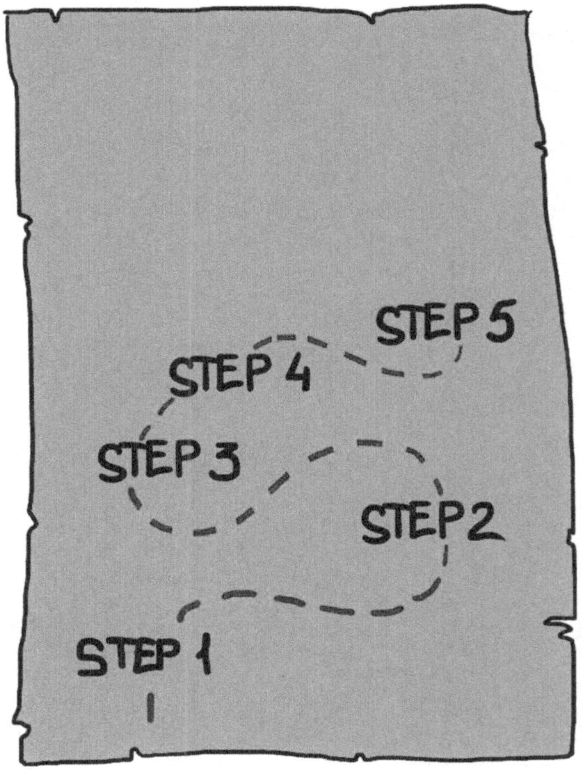

STEP 5: MAKING THE EPIC SHIFT

What is great in man is that he is a bridge and not an end.

—Friedrich Nietzsche

The next stop on my worldwide adventure was Thailand, where some of the world's oldest and most powerful inner world navigation strategies are rooted in twenty-five hundred years of Buddhist philosophy and meditation practice. After a brief stop in Bangkok acclimating to a brand new world, the flow of Silence guided me toward Stillness, pulling northward. I trekked to Chiang Mai, a popular passageway between the hustle of Bangkok and Thailand's virtually untouched mountains. I couldn't wait to see what I'd discover.

Or, at least, I mostly couldn't wait.

Thailand had just experienced a violent coup d'etat, wherein the military overthrew the government. Even though the world's oldest known moat surrounds Chiang Mai's old city, cocooning it from the surrounding world, military troops still occupied Chiang Mai's main square.

I came to Thailand expecting to absorb a culture that deeply values inner world mastery. Some of that was unmistakable: The awareness of being connected to all of humanity was deeply felt by the community as a whole, rather than being a shared intellectual exercise. I could instantly sense that people were steeped in the flow of Silence. In individual interactions, I was surrounded by kindness and patience. Just looking into people's faces helped me connect to Silence. What a warm, welcoming place!

And yet, the air was full of uncertainty and risk, raising my inner awareness threat-level to high alert. When alone, unfamiliar sounds, gestures, and scents constantly distracted me. I repeatedly had to remind myself that changes in the outer world were impacting the dialogue in my inner world.

One day, walking out of a restaurant, I heard a loud bang. Adrenaline shot through my blood. Fear flooded my inner world. An instant later, a second loud burst erupted behind me. I ducked, turning quickly. Fright and defensive instincts collided on my Bridge of Translation, and terrified thoughts flew off of it, producing a SELF of defense and isolation.

I was primed for fear, and my inner world was overwhelmed by my automatic, instinctual emotions.

As I turned, a child's laughing face caught my eye. Confused, my mind raced to process the outer world. I swiveled to look around, unsure of what to expect. And then I saw a massive parade turning the corner behind me. A single drummer led the way with a very large drum. As I watched him beat the drum, I could hear the deep booms of his instrument repeat. I exhaled, smiling back at the child, relieved.

In the next second, I took a deep breath and reminded myself that I was on a journey through Silence to Stillness. I let myself feel Silence's flow, and I watched as my inner dialogue quieted. Fear no longer controlled the SELF arising from my bridge; I was again connected with Silence.

Once again in control of my inner world, I'd done something huge. In fact, it's so huge that I call it the Epic Shift. Today, I'm going to teach you the three steps that create this powerful skill in key moments.

KEY MOMENTS

That heart-stopping moment when I thought I was caught in the middle of a politically motivated gunfight? That is a perfect example of a *key moment*—a moment when our inner world reactions push us out of our emotional comfort zone. My *key moment trigger*—its catalyst—was the percussive boom from the parade.

Key moments are the times when an outer world experience creates an automatic inner world reaction that pushes us out of our emotional comfort zone.

Our outer world environments influence our inner world experiences. Key moments, and key moment triggers, illustrate that relationship so clearly. The provocative image Mind Exercise that you just completed provided you with the experience of a key moment—your emotional upheaval as you viewed a meaningful outer world picture.

For people who have not intentionally visited their inner world, key moment triggers almost always push you into an uncomfortable emotional state. While triggers are individual, we all have them and we have habitually ingrained reactions to them. Perhaps you feel shame after being ignored; someone else might feel angry; another person may not be triggered at all. But everyone feels emotional discomfort at times.

As with the provocative image, all key moments alter your inner world and your subsequent inner dialogue—even though you may not be consciously aware of the changes, or even that a key moment trigger occurred. Listening closely to the changes in your inner dialogue immediately after a key moment trigger can be supremely challenging. It's also one of the most important skills that you can practice to make changes in your brain, body, and life.

Key moments mark a transition in your inner world, when your thoughts and their related emotions are both close to the Bridge of Translation. This makes them available for your conscious observation and simultaneous consideration.

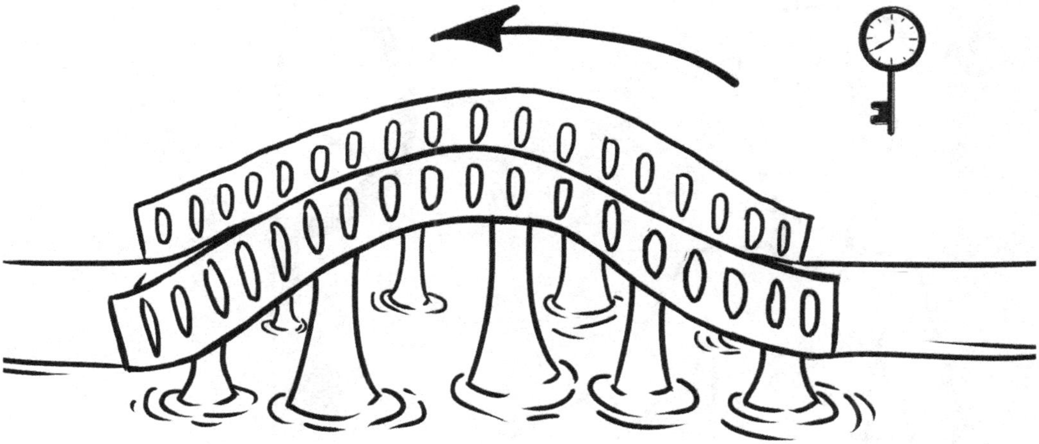

Key moments allow you to observe thoughts and their related emotions on the Bridge of Translation.

Key moments, when observed in real time, give us a choice about how to respond to them in our inner world.

When we can recognize key moments, we can make a choice. With practice, you can turn your emotional discomfort into progress on your personal inner world path.

THE EPIC SHIFT

Making a choice about our inner world dialogue is the basis of the Epic Shift, a key element of completing your journey to Stillness. The Epic Shift is simply this: listening to your inner dialogue while having a specific intention in mind.

You make the Epic Shift by choosing to listen to your inner dialogue with a specific intention in mind.

The Epic Shift only takes three simple steps; it's amazing that so few people realize that something so important boils down to something so achievable. If you can consistently implement these steps, you can make the Epic Shift on demand, any time you notice that you've lost connection from Silence.

1. Recall your intention of making an inner world journey through Silence to Stillness.
2. Notice Silence flowing through your body.
3. Listen to your inner dialogue until it has quieted back into connection with Silence.

Clearly understanding the key insight behind the Epic Shift allows us to move ever more strategically through the inner world. However, we cannot reach our intended destination—Stillness—without consistently implementing the shift. When we can do that, our brains, bodies, and emotional lives all are changed, and we can go the rest of the way to Stillness.

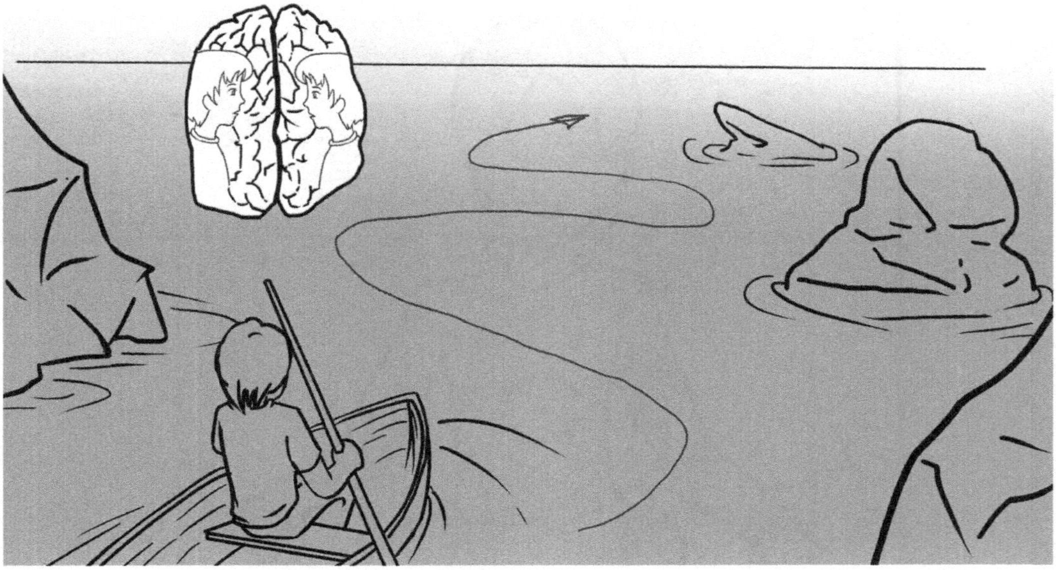

The Epic Shift is required to take you the rest of the way to Stillness.

In previous Mind Exercises, you've come to identify precisely what Silence is turning into as it flows into and through your brain and body. You've listened as Silence morphs into arising SELFs and as it flows into instincts, impulses, and emotions. Becoming your purpose also includes knowing how to *direct* Silence's transformation.

As you more clearly hear the words and see the distractions that flow off your Bridge of Translation, you increase your skill at strategically navigating through your inner world toward Stillness. Making the Epic Shift is the foundation of this skill.

When you make the Epic Shift today, I want you to actually *feel* the inner world change that occurs. Experience with crystal clarity that you are directing your life each moment as you control the traffic on your Bridge of Translation. You are navigating your inner world and directing the SELF that arises.

Take a moment now to make the Epic Shift for the first time. Observe how your inner world changes.

1. Recall your intention of making an inner world journey through Silence to Stillness.
2. Notice Silence flowing through your body.
3. Listen to your inner dialogue until it has quieted back into connection with Silence.

Do you feel the change in your inner world? You may only experience a subtle shift at first. You'll continue to notice the inner world change strengthening as you consistently make the Epic Shift.

WHY IT WORKS

New brain science has shown that making the Epic Shift when you get frustrated *today* is an effective way to change how you will react to *future* frustrations. That's because you are making actual changes to the way your brain (and body) processes information and, so, how you experience your life.

Making the Epic Shift consistently changes the structure and function of millions of cells inside your brain and body. (Conversely, when you fail to consistently make the Epic Shift, your brain cells will revert to old patterns of inner dialogue, and your journey to Stillness will stall.)

Recognizing both the physical and mental impact of your journey underscores the power of making the Epic Shift consistently.

Inner world masters in Thailand have known this for centuries: An effective way to change how Silence will flow through you (and into your world of tomorrow) is to notice, and then shift, what your inner world is producing right now. For thousands of years in the East, they have strategically listened and used thoughts, imagination, and a deep connection to Silence to process emotional content, to navigate, and to make changes to their SELF. Only more recently has the Western world become captivated by Eastern inner world practices.

In the twentieth century, many Western scientists traveled east, developed personal meditation practices, and then researched, wrote, and taught widely about what they learned and experienced. Similarly, accomplished inner world masters from the East traveled West and shared their expertise.

The resulting intellectual and cultural momentum led to Western-trained brain scientists joining with Buddhism's spiritual leader, the Dalai Lama, to research the impact of meditation on our brain, body, and experience of life. In the epitome of Western science joining with Eastern wisdom, Buddhist monks laid down in high-tech functional magnetic resonance imaging (fMRI) machines to have their brains scanned as they meditated (i.e., Mind Exercised).

The Western researchers set out to measure whether any physical changes had actually occurred in the monks' brains as a result of all that meditation. The empirical research demonstrated for the first time that strategically exercising the brain had created significant observable and measurable brain changes.

In other words, intentional Mind Exercise allows you to physically change your brain—both in structure and in function.

This Western "discovery" has launched a different epic shift in the scientific understanding of how our brains and our SELFs develop and change throughout life. Brain science now has hard data that illustrates the physical power of consistent and intentional navigation through the inner world.

TRANSFORM YOUR LIFE

The second half of *Be Your Purpose* ensures you learn to notice when it's time to make the Epic Shift—and then hone your ability to do so. By making the Epic Shift, you are strategically changing how Silence is flowing through you.

When you make the Epic Shift, you physically and mentally transform your life.

How Silence transforms as it flows through you dictates your experience of life and seeds each experience of tomorrow. As you transform Silence's flow, you are transforming your inner and outer life experience—relationships, lifestyle, everything you direct your attention to in the outer world.

Because Silence is constantly transforming as it flows through the contents of your inner world and back into the outer world, even making a simple inner dialogue change has significant ripple effects. By changing your inner dialogue to be more peaceful in the moment, the Silence that leaves your body reflects this change and shapes everything you encounter in the outer world in a more peaceful way.

Moving forward, your full-time task is to remain aware of your inner world. Recognize whatever is distracting your awareness from the Silence flowing through you. As you observe and make changes to your inner world, you will bring experiences into your life that could not possibly have occurred for you before.

Your Step 5 Mind Exercise will continue to expand your ability to notice when you get distracted and will begin to develop your capacity to redirect the Silence flowing through you. When you intentionally trigger, and then observe, a key moment, you'll take another step toward bringing personal arising key moments into your conscious awareness, where you can make choices as to whether and how to respond to them.

Wherever I am, Silence flows through me.

Wherever you are, Silence flows through you.

Ready to practice listening to and shifting the flow of Silence?

Let's go.

THE DAILY RITUAL

Begin today's Mind Exercise by completing the Daily Ritual (starting with five minutes of physical exercise) located in Appendix A. When you have completed the Daily Ritual, return here to complete your Step 5 Mind Exercise. *You may access a video version of the Daily Ritual and Step 5 Mind Exercise at BeYourPurpose.com.*

Done with the Daily Ritual and ready to continue with your Step 5 Mind Exercise?

Good work. Let's keep going.

MIND EXERCISE

Making the Epic Shift

WELCOME TO YOUR STEP 5 MIND EXERCISE!

Invite a key moment onto your Bridge of Translation and increase the intensity of conscious processing occurring on your bridge.

Read the italicized paragraph below, which will consciously trigger your inner world. As you close your eyes for one minute, recognize the key moment that accepts your invitation and arises onto your bridge. (You'll know the key moment has occurred when you experience an unpleasant inner world sensation or impulse that makes you doubt your abilities. It may feel like the weather on your bridge has darkened.)

When this happens, do not become distracted away from your awareness of Silence or become fused to the thoughts, emotions, or stories that may begin to arise in your inner world. Instead, as soon as you notice that your inner world has been triggered, take notice of the event and immediately make the Epic Shift, following the instructions included below.

Ready to listen to your inner world and make the Epic Shift?

Go.

I invite any conscious or unconscious beliefs I maintain about my own limitations onto my bridge. And I invite any and all related impulses, thoughts, emotions, or pains that hold me back from recognizing or being my purpose. Be they memories, fears, betrayals, failures, or shame, I invite them onto my bridge for conscious inspection now.

Did you notice what arose in your inner world?

Good.

Now, make the Epic Shift.

1. Recall your intention of making an inner world journey through Silence to Stillness.
2. Notice Silence flowing through your body.
3. Listen to your inner dialogue until it has quieted back into connection with Silence.

How does your inner world feel right now?

Is your inner world calm again? If your inner world still feels triggered at all, repeat the steps to make the Epic Shift until you are connected to Silence again.

Feeling Silence?

Great.

In the space below, make notes about what arose in your inner world before you made the Epic Shift. There are no wrong answers, but your notes will help you to complete future Mind Exercises.

My Inner World Reaction

By intentionally triggering a key moment and making the Epic Shift back to a calm inner world, you've made a massive surge forward in your journey to Stillness. When you remember to make the Epic Shift, inner world distractions no longer derail your journey. Instead, you choose to use these distractions to train your brain and body to move toward Stillness. Each time you practice recovering from emotional stumbles, you reduce the time spent in doubt or turmoil and your journey accelerates.

You've completed Step 5, *and* you're now halfway through *Be Your Purpose*.
Congratulations!

The second half will feel even more personal, and you'll begin noticing inner world activity in real time throughout your days. By making the Epic Shift each time distractions arise, you'll bring your inner dialogue further into your awareness. To move all the way to Stillness, however, you must commit to tracking your inner dialogue vigilantly and to making the Epic Shift consistently.

To support that process, build a new habit: Notice your first few thoughts of the day. Your first thoughts typically occur before you've even opened your eyes. Each day, take note of these thoughts and then immediately make the Epic Shift. You'll deepen your connection to Silence and reorient yourself to your journey to Stillness.

In our next step, you'll learn to consider the key moment triggers that have become encased in your inner world through the course of your life.

Congratulations again on your progress.

I'll see you again when you're ready to continue.

STEP 6

Uncovering Personal Triggers

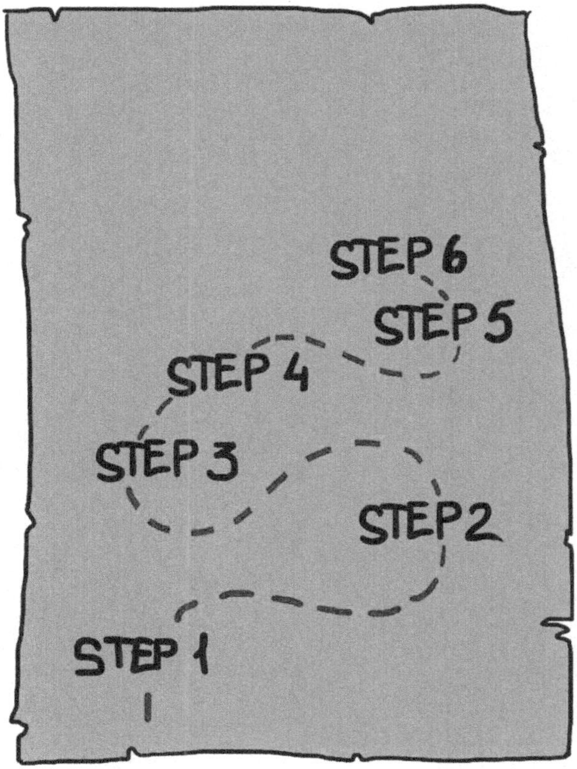

STEP 6: UNCOVERING PERSONAL TRIGGERS

Allow the book to do its work, to awaken you from the old grooves of your repetitive and conditioned thinking.

—Eckhart Tolle

After a couple days in Chiang Mai, I found an Internet café where I could check my email. I went in with my fingers crossed. My bank account was dwindling. I hoped I'd hear from a book publisher with a hefty advance. I really really really *really* hoped I'd hear. I'd never been good with financial uncertainty.

Unfortunately, I didn't have an email from a book publisher. What a letdown. No, it was more than that—I felt devastated. My mind raced through the numbers. Did I have enough money to finish my trip? Would I be able to afford rent when I got home, let alone pay off credit cards and loans? How was I going to start seeing patients again without money for an office? *This is embarrassing and scary,* I thought. *I can't even tell anyone.*

I checked my account balance from the café. The numbers hadn't magically increased since my last visit. My mind replayed stories of friends and patients who had lost their jobs. Images of bills with "PAST DUE" stamped in angry red letters on them flashed over my bridge. My heartbeat accelerated. I disconnected from the computer so as not to add to my miniscule internet café usage change. I had to sit still there for a while though.

My mind and body let the emotional uncertainty take over.

It took over an hour before I realized what had happened that day. I'd let a longstanding fear derail my journey to Stillness. Within seconds, my inner world was overwhelmed with turmoil, and my whole body responded—my mind, my heart, even my legs gave in to the emotions that were triggered.

When I finally realized what had happened, I took a deep breath. I recalled my intention to journey through Silence to Stillness. I once again noticed Silence flowing through my body. And I listened as my inner dialogue quieted back into connection with Silence.

Sound familiar? I made the Epic Shift—but I made it an hour after the trigger. Unlike at the parade, where I noticed the key moment and immediately responded with the Epic Shift, this time I was emotionally provoked so jarringly that I lost my connection with Silence—and the resulting upheaval distracted me from that connection for far longer.

As I finally listened to Silence again, I thought about how quickly old fears—in this case, fear of financial problems—can overwhelm us. I experienced the power of *key moment trigger events* and their ability to pull you into a whirlpool of a mistaken SELF.

KEY MOMENT TRIGGER EVENTS

Key moment trigger events are really just a subset of key moment triggers; however, they are the most potent—the types of events through which *you* are most vulnerable to being emotionally provoked and/or distracted away from Silence. They can be sparked by the outer world or the inner world. Wherever they originate, they pull you out of your emotional comfort zone, to a place where you can lose the connection to Silence.

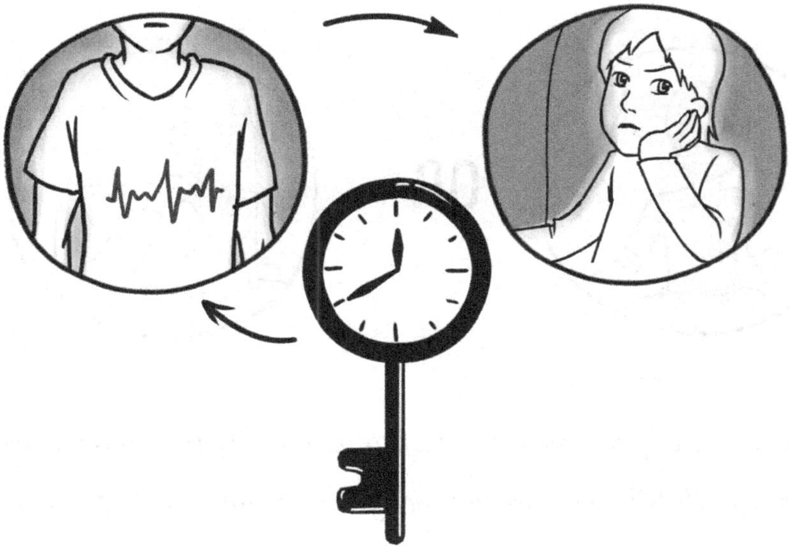

A key moment trigger event distracts you from Silence by shifting you out of your emotional comfort zone.

In the last Mind Exercises, you experienced how easily memories and beliefs can trigger your inner world. When these triggers are related to deeply held, longstanding beliefs or emotionally charged past events, they are key moment trigger events. When a key moment trigger event occurs, your Bridge of Translation reacts defensively.

You see, each bridge has a set of rules for translating information, and there is a very specific rule about responding to possible threats in your environment, honed through millennia of surviving perilous circumstances: Your bridge rapidly and automatically prepares for danger. By default, your bridge will produce a version of your SELF, mistaken or not, that your history suggests is necessary (based on the colliding traffic of emotions and instincts and impulses) to return to emotional and physical safety. It's the proverbial fight-or-flight response.

A key moment trigger event is seen as a threat, and your Bridge of Translation reacts as such—even though no real danger may exist. This leads to an especially powerful moment of transition.

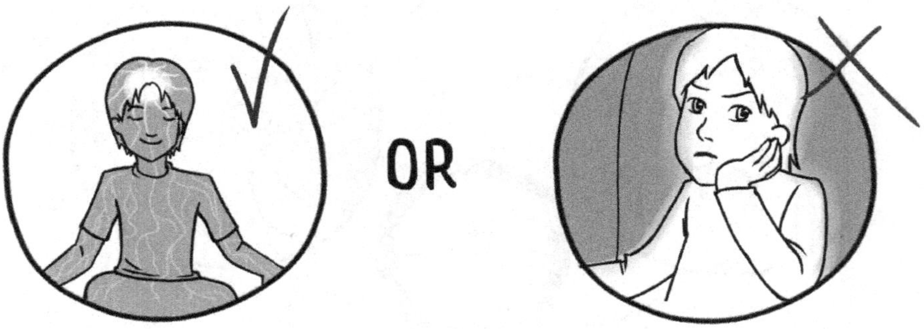

Key moment trigger events are an opportunity to choose a deeper bond with Silence—or to sever your connection to Silence.

Essentially, they are emotional forks in the rivers of your inner world—opportunities that you'll learn to use as a guide to Stillness. Just as with any key moment trigger, when you can notice key moment trigger events in real time, you can make a choice about your responses to them. You can choose one fork, which leads to the Epic Shift and forward towards Stillness. Or you can allow old momentum to pulled you down the other fork, which leads to distracting emotions, thoughts, and stories that direct you away from Stillness.

Increasing your capacity to notice key moment trigger events in real time is how you bring them into your conscious awareness when they occur, so you can choose how you'll respond. With practice, you'll train your key moment trigger events to provoke the Epic Shift.

The first step towards that is uncovering the key moment trigger events that are most common for you, which we'll do in today's Mind Exercise. As you practice noticing these events, you'll continue training yourself to make the Epic Shift whenever they occur—rather than taking the other fork, which I call being pulled into the whirlpool of a mistaken SELF.

THE WHIRLPOOL OF A MISTAKEN SELF

When you get sucked into a whirlpool of a mistaken SELF, you become possessed by old, conditioned, mistaken patterns of SELF. Rather than recognizing your momentary lapse in awareness, you amp up your inner world reaction to the trigger event. Your Bridge of Translation is flooded with extra activity, and your connection to Silence diminishes.

This extra activity reinforces old habits and inner dialogue patterns. You lose awareness of your inner world, and therefore you forget that you have the freedom to choose how you'll cope with the situation. It's as though you are being pulled under water, yet you forget to swim toward the air.

A whirlpool of a mistaken SELF diminishes, or even severs, your connection to Silence.

Unfortunately, when you are pulled into a whirlpool of a mistaken SELF, you increase the likelihood of being pulled into the same whirlpool in the future. Your ability to cope with a similar situation next time it arises is compromised. If a particular key moment trigger event pushes you into the whirlpool of a mistaken SELF—especially if you stay there, unaware that you've left the path to Stillness—then you're extremely vulnerable to becoming that mistaken SELF whenever that trigger event reoccurs.

The good news is that, even after you've become a mistaken SELF, you *always* have another chance to make the Epic Shift. You just have to notice that you have been distracted from your path to Stillness. Straying from the path usually appears in the form of excessive thinking, painful emotions, blaming others, or even physical pain.

When you realize that you are in a whirlpool, you can take a deep breath and remember your intention. It doesn't matter if you've been stuck in your old patterns of a mistaken SELF for minutes, hours, or even days. You can make the Epic Shift simply by remembering your intention and moving through the three steps until your inner world quiets. With a little practice, you'll discover that you have the capacity to reconnect to Silence and continue your journey to Stillness anytime.

You can always return to your path toward Stillness.

WHY IT WORKS

Your key moment trigger events have been part of your life for a long time. Which means you've probably spent years being pulled into whirlpools. Your reactions to these trigger events have repeatedly recurred in your inner world, and you no longer even notice the persistent interruptions to your connection to Silence. Whirlpools are thoroughly integrated into how your bridge functions and into the resulting, broader, inner world cellular reaction.

With such deeply ingrained emotional reactions, you may think mistaken SELFs are simply "you." Your reactions are not you though! They are old brain-body habits—i.e., brain-body cell networks that are connected in a way that distracts you from deepening your awareness of and connection to Silence flowing through you.

When you face the emotional fork caused by a key moment trigger event, it's always easier—automatic, even—to "choose" the whirlpool of a mistaken SELF. It's the default based on years of old brain habits, and following that route reinforces old brain habits.

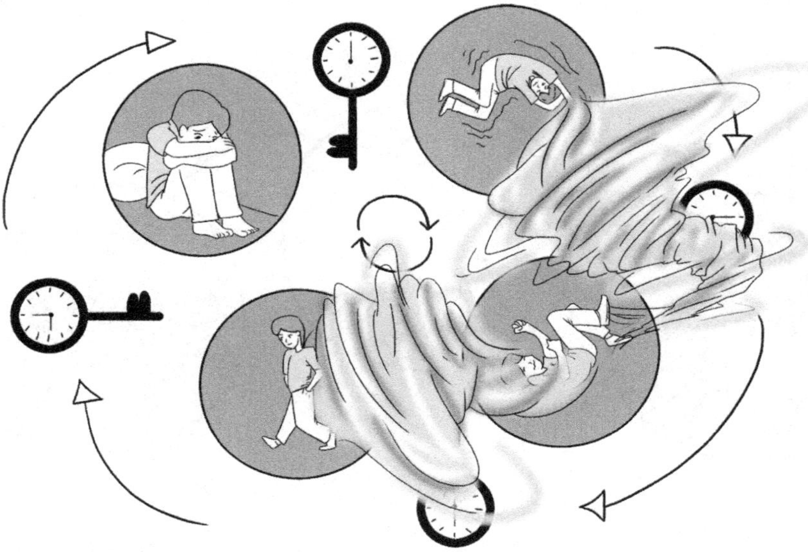

However, when you are aware of the fork and you consciously choose to make the Epic Shift, you start to break the old habit. As you consistently make the Epic Shift in these moments, you then create new brain habits. You rebuild the pathways in your brain, and your brain will increase its capacity to reconnect to Silence in the face of any trigger.

Of course, key moment trigger events are difficult to observe in real time because your entrenched brain cell networks have been wired to automatically react to these triggers at the moment they occur. If you cannot identify them, your bridge will continue to prepare for danger in these moments. To retrain your bridge's overprotective reactions, you must learn to identify your key moment trigger events—the events that most persistently provoke your inner world.

Again, once you identify these old brain habits, you can break them and build new ones. In this case, you'll build a habit of making the Epic Shift. With practice, you'll become a master of identifying your personal key moment trigger events and automatically making the Epic Shift.

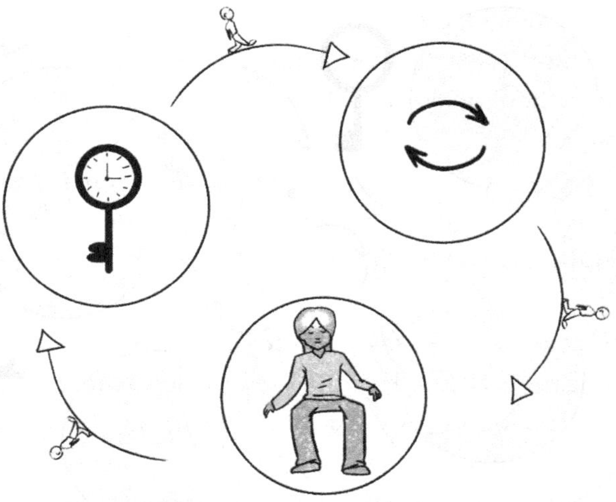

You will master a new brain habit that deepens your connection to Silence and brings you closer to Stillness.

To truly interrupt your journey to Stillness, a key moment trigger event must completely sever your connection to the Silence flowing through you. It needs to actually suck you into a whirlpool of a mistaken SELF. As you work through today's Mind Exercise, you will begin the process of rewiring your brain so that you automatically navigate your inner world around the dangers of whirlpools.

ALLOW YOURSELF A WANDERING PATH

No journey to Stillness is straight. Everyone gets triggered and distracted. In Chiang Mai, I was immersed in an unfamiliar world. You, too, are surrounded by sounds, sights, smells, and emerging situations. Some of these are familiar, and some are jarring. Our senses are bombarded by inner and outer world stimulation all day, everyday.

The constant barrage of information requires us to make split-second inner world adjustments. You'll make millions of these decisions throughout your life, sculpting your brain, your inner dialogue, and your path through the outer world along the way. Some of these decisions will be intentional and beneficial. Some of these decisions will not.

Allow yourself this wandering path. As you move forward, you'll train yourself to notice arising key moment trigger events and continue your journey toward Stillness. Some days you will train more effectively than others, but you can always return to the path.

It starts with our new habit of taking note of the first thoughts of the day. I hope you remembered to begin this and then follow your observation by making the Epic Shift. Each day you do this, you begin your day by sculpting your inner dialogue in line with your conscious intentions.

Today, you will move closer to Stillness as you increase your capacity to identify and more automatically recognize your personal key moment trigger events. You are arming yourself with the ability to rebound emotionally from life's constant challenges, no matter what you are faced with, no matter where your journey weaves.

Ready to begin identifying your personal key moment trigger events and build new brain habits?

Let's go.

THE DAILY RITUAL

Begin today's Mind Exercise by completing the Daily Ritual (starting with five minutes of physical exercise) located in Appendix A. When you have completed the Daily Ritual, return here to complete your Step 6 Mind Exercise. *You may access a video version of the Daily Ritual and Step 6 Mind Exercise at BeYourPurpose.com.*

Done with the Daily Ritual and ready to continue with your Step 6 Mind Exercise?

Good work. Let's keep going.

MIND EXERCISE

Uncovering Personal Triggers

Welcome to your STEP 6 Mind Exercise!

Uncover your personal vulnerabilities to being distracted and the triggers that can send you into a whirlpool of a mistaken SELF. You'll begin training yourself to respond differently to these triggers.

Before you can strategically change your automatic reactions to your key moment trigger events, you need to become familiar with what your personal habitually recurring triggers are. These are the ones that you must know about and master to progress on your journey to Stillness. In today's Mind Exercise, you will make a private list of the types of moments that have triggered you in the last month.

What has thrown you off your game in the last month? What recent events provoked you to intense emotions like anger or sadness, or to lose your motivation, or to feel disconnected from life? What old wounds are you reminded of most often? Does anything make you withdraw from friends, family, or other parts of life? Are there specific worries that stop you from pursuing something purposeful that you'd planned to do? The answers to these questions are all key moment trigger events.

Take a few moments right now to make a list of your top five most recent key moment trigger events. A good place to begin may be by recalling the key moment that arose for you during your previous Mind Exercises. If you need help creating your list, repeat the Step 5 Mind Exercise to invite triggers into your inner world.

My Five Biggest Key Moment Trigger Events

1. ______________________________

2. ______________________________

3. ______________________________

4. ______________________________

5. ______________________________

I've included my list below to give you an example of some personal key moment triggers.

Sean's Biggest Key Moment Trigger Events

1. Feeling lied to or abandoned
2. Money matters – talking or thinking about them
3. Waiting for "important" news
4. Listening to criticism about someone I love
5. Thinking about or giving tough love

Done making your list?

Good work!

Now, invite in and experience the most provocative element from your list—your *primary key moment trigger event.* After you invite your primary trigger onto your bridge, notice yourself shifting emotionally toward the whirlpool. Immediately make the Epic Shift back into connection with Silence.

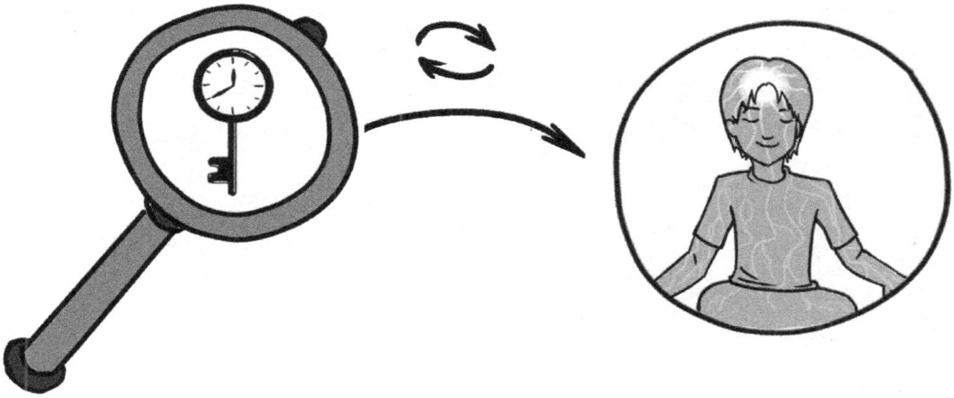

Ready to invite the most provocative key moment trigger event into your inner world, and then make the Epic Shift?

Go.

When you're ready, follow the three steps below to make the Epic Shift back into connection with Silence.

1. Recall your intention of making an inner world journey through Silence to Stillness.
2. Notice Silence flowing through your body.
3. Listen to your inner dialogue until it has quieted back into connection with Silence.

Feeling calm?

Good.

By uncovering your most ubiquitous triggers, and then strategically provoking your primary key moment trigger event before making the Epic Shift, you've taken another significant step along your journey to Stillness.

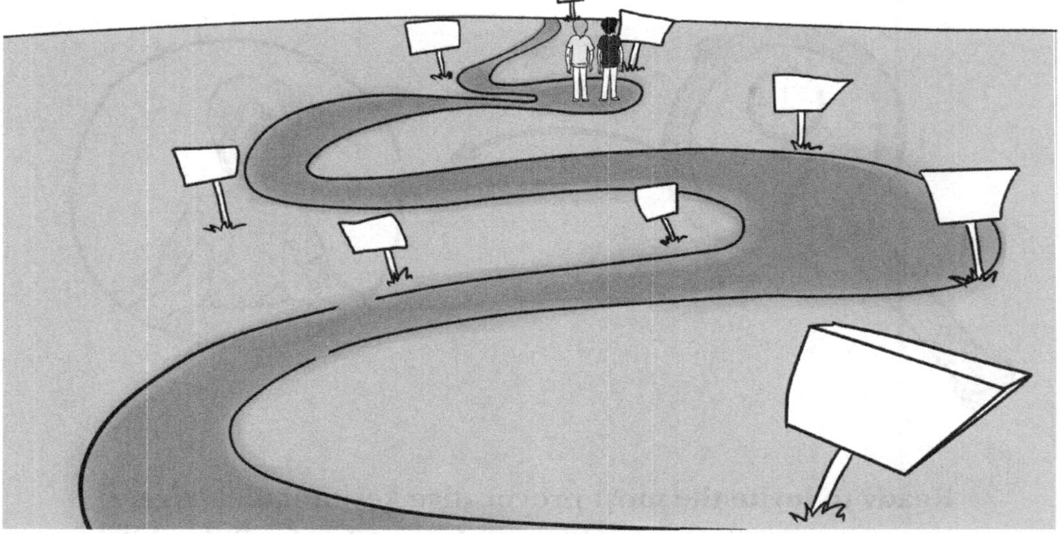

You've completed Step 6.
Congratulations!

Rest well now. Step 7 is frequently the most challenging step on the journey to Stillness. You'll uncover what has held you back from being your purpose throughout your life. You'll be more honest with yourself than you ever have been before.

I'll see you again when you're ready to continue.

STEP 7

Identifying Your Biggest Obstacle

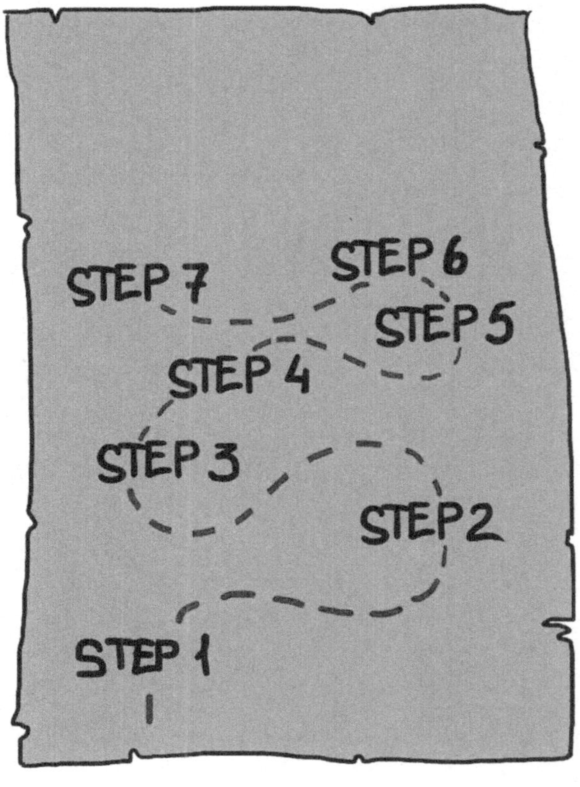

STEP 7: IDENTIFYING YOUR BIGGEST OBSTACLE

Hold the sadness and pain of samsara in your heart and at the same time the power and vision of the Great Eastern Sun. Then the warrior can make a proper cup of tea.

—Chogyam Trengpa Rinpoche

After a week in Chiang Mai, I slipped my backpack on and hopped on a motorbike. I began the trek to a storied Thai valley oasis called Pai through hundreds of hairpin turns, steep mountain grades, and uneven terrain. An hour in and still three hours from Pai, a thunderstorm hit. The road slickened.

Veering left, I squeezed the brakes to slow down. My tires spun through roadside mud. I lost control of the bike, hit an embankment, and flew over the handlebars. The bike landed in a ditch. I landed harder, bouncing on the concrete before stopping.

I lay bleeding and drenching, alone on a nameless Thai mountain road. The skin over my hip was torn raw through layers of shredded clothes. The entire left side of my body stung. My ribs stabbed with pain. It was hard to breathe.

There was no help. So I got up.

The bike was damaged but still started. I drove out of the ditch and slowly made my way through the downpour back toward Chiang Mai. Thirty minutes later, with supplies from a 7-Eleven, I poured rubbing alcohol over each open wound and bandaged myself. I've never experienced sharper physical pain than I did finishing the ride back.

Laying in bed that night, I reflected on my journey and choices. Leaving on this journey had taken a leap of faith, a belief in and commitment to my purpose that meant overcoming my fears. That night, my fears rushed back in. I felt scared and alone.

I had no money in the bank and no book advance. Everything I owned was in a ten-foot-by-ten-foot storage container on the other side of the world. The last conversation with my mom consisted of her quizzing me about my life choices (especially my lack of a wife, children, and "real" job). The validity of her concerns, in my mind, was underscored by the thoughts of Aleksandra, the woman I'd left behind and whom I thought could be The One…if only I were near her.

Shaken up, I began to see an old version of my SELF return. (You'll remember meeting this version of my SELF before.) Sure enough, the scared little boy inside me, uncertainly dipping one foot in a pool of water, then suddenly frozen still, had made the trip overseas with me. The scared little boy consumed my attention and interrupted my connection to the flow of Silence through me.

The frozen boy in me is personified fear. When "threats" loom large—especially my primary key moment trigger event—he rushes to my Bridge of Translation. My true SELF retreats, and the scared little boy blocks my evolving path of purpose.

In Chiang Mai, the scared little boy had not only returned, but he steered me into the whirlpool of a mistaken SELF. From there, I spiraled into a predictable cycle of thoughts, emotions, and behaviors. It was the worst possible scenario for my inner world. I'd allowed the whirlpool, combined with uncertainty, memory, and old habits of mind, to provoke a *SELF-defeating cycle.*

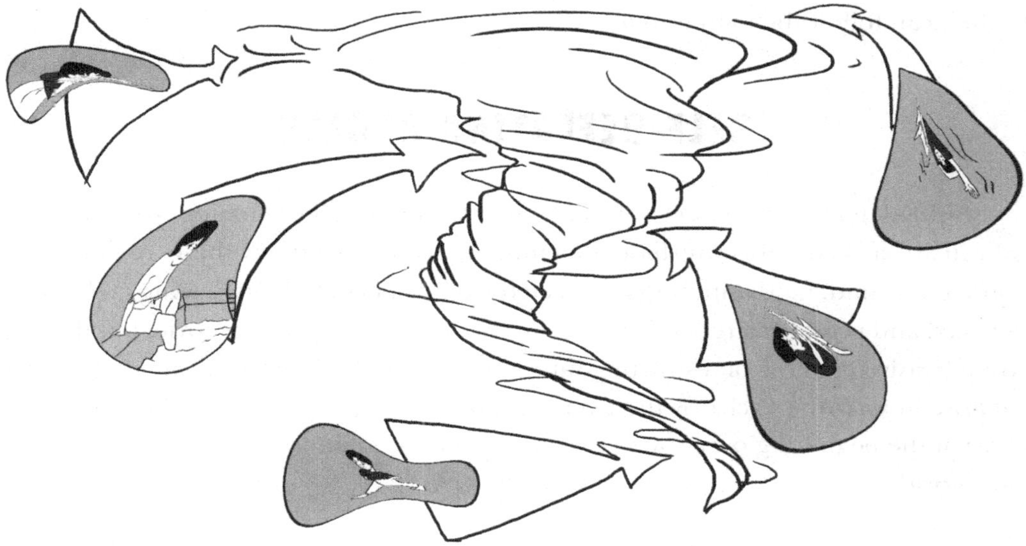

It took me more time than I'd like to admit, but I was able to stop my SELF-defeating cycle. That's because I had an advantage: I'd seen this particular version of my SELF arise so many times before that I'd developed a strategy to ensure I'd recognize him whenever he arose in the future. I created an image of what he looks like in my imagination.

When I recognized that I had ceded my journey to the scared little boy, I could uninvite him from my inner world. I made the Epic Shift, and I made the choice to return to my evolving path to purpose. I recommitted to seeing my journey through.

Soon, I received a message from Aleksandra: "I love the idea of your return, of there being more to see and feel and do together. Whatever it is that planted the seed for this trip, I'm grateful for it." Shortly thereafter, I got an email from a book agent asking to schedule a phone call. And when my mom and I talked again a few weeks later, she apologized. She told me that she loved me and that she was proud that I always followed my heart. I told her how much I loved her too, and then I said it wasn't my heart I was following. It was Silence.

Just as I was, you too will be challenged, distracted, discouraged, filled with doubt, and drawn off your path in a thousand thoughts as you complete your journey to Stillness. How we respond to losses, setbacks, and fear is what defines our life. But if we can name our SELF-defeating cycles, we can build a sure-fire strategy for navigating the most challenging inner world distractions that arise along the journey to Stillness. We then can follow the path to purpose.

SELF-DEFEATING CYCLES

SELF-defeating cycles occur when you fail to notice a key moment trigger event, and you are sucked into a whirlpool of a mistaken SELF—and stay there. As you go round and round, increasingly disconnected from Silence, SELF-defeating cycles are provoked and produce a repetitive inner movie. Not just any inner movie, but the most pervasive patterns of distracting inner world thoughts, emotions, and behaviors that arise in *you.* Your cycles by their very nature are self-perpetuating: They naturally restart at the beginning over and over again, just as this pattern repeats in your inner world.

When you're in a SELF-defeating cycle, your inner world returns to the same inner movie over and over again.

SELF-defeating cycles are dead-ends on the map of your inner world. Think of them like rivulets that peter out in a swamp of muck. Even worse, if you are in a SELF-defeating cycle, you continually circle the edge of this dead-end. As if asleep in your craft, you don't even try to escape. Meanwhile, your mistaken SELF gets louder: "There's no way out! You can't get anywhere else!" he shouts. It's a major barrier to deepening your connection to Silence.

Keep in mind that life will always challenge your connection to Silence. Sometimes it only takes a subtle change in your environment to displace your intention. Sometimes major changes in your life reactivate an old version of your SELF. In these moments, your inner world space may diminish. You may find it difficult to see the changes within the broader context of your life.

When you lose that awareness, you fall into a SELF-defeating cycle. Stuck at an inner world dead-end, your outer world takes on a distorted sense of importance. You will often fixate on an aspect of your life that is in conflict with the intention of being your purpose. You become absorbed by a mistaken SELF's most power-sapping narratives.

Ironically, what you "hear" often sounds like you are trying to care for your SELF. Narratives usually aim at either defending your SELF's imagined territory or plotting to claim more SELF importance. "I can't trust anyone! I'm all by myself. Nothing matters." Through it all, your SELF-defeating cycle remains transparent to you.

No surprise, not knowing that you've become stuck in a SELF-defeating cycle is an obstacle to recovering your connection to Silence. You suffer from inner blindness that shifts you off your path to Stillness and obscures your view—and you have no clue that you have strayed.

For this reason, recognizing your SELF-defeating cycles when they arise is essential to navigating to Stillness. Just like in the outer world, when you realize that you're at a dead-end, you can navigate back to your chosen path.

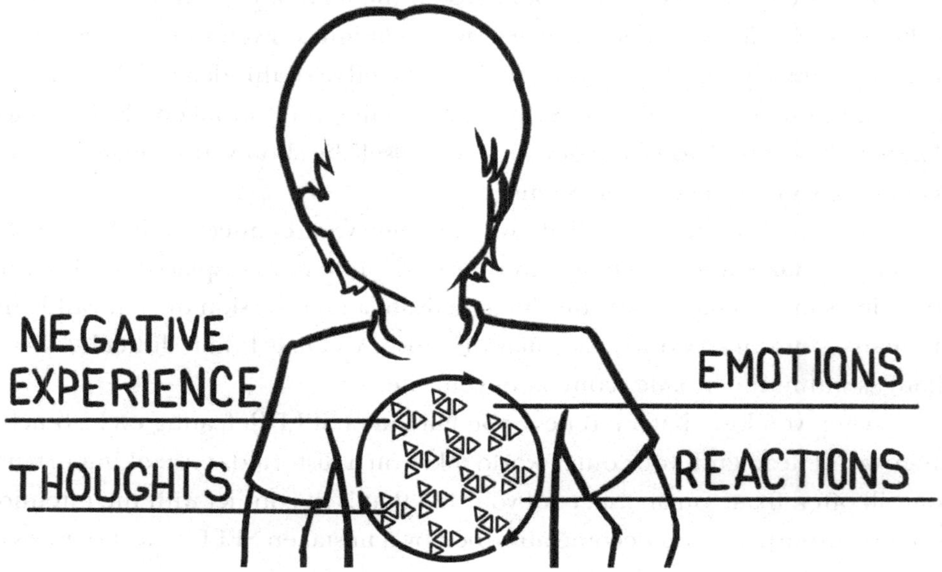

You will identify the patterns of your primary SELF-defeating cycle, so you can navigate to Stillness.

In this Mind Exercise, you'll identify your biggest inner world obstacle—your primary SELF-defeating cycle. You will unravel the patterns of your habitual negative experiences, thoughts, emotions, and reactions that are its foundation. By learning to clear your primary SELF-defeating cycle from your path, you'll become able to unravel and overcome any obstacle you encounter along the remainder of your journey to Stillness. You will have cleared the inner world path to being your purpose.

Learn to navigate through fear and the deceptive "ease" of your SELF's habitual reactions.

YOUR PRIMARY SELF-DEFEATING CYCLE

None of us are immune from developing or returning to SELF-defeating cycles from time to time. Our lives are filled with losses provoked by events that are out of our control. For example, injuries, illness, disabilities, your own history of memories and pains, both old and new, are fundamental aspects of human life.

Today you'll see, capture, tame, and silence your primary SELF-defeating cycle. This is your most common SELF-defeating cycle, the pattern of inner world distractions that most quickly arises when you are faced with a key moment trigger event. It is your biggest inner world obstacle. Spiraling out of view just behind your eyes, your primary SELF-defeating cycle has repeated over and over throughout your life.

Once you've clearly seen your primary SELF-defeating cycle, however, you'll understand how to identify any SELF-defeating cycle that emerges in your inner world. When you can see your SELF-defeating cycles, you can master them: You can tame them and transform your SELF back into connection with Silence. You'll be able to notice and transform any SELF-defeating cycle that threatens progress along your journey to Stillness.

Recognizing your primary SELF-defeating cycle can be difficult when you are deep within it, but as you read this, you probably have some inklings. If you were to observe yourself objectively from a distance, which postures and reactions would you see repeated frequently? How do you react in moments that feel threatening to you? These are the unconscious SELF-defeating versions of your SELF—the "you" that you become when you remain stuck in a whirlpool of a mistaken SELF.

What shape(s), emotion(s), and inner image(s) does your SELF habitually project when you get really triggered? Here are some questions that may help you:

- Do you become shy like a wallflower or withdraw?
- Do you become angry or lash out like a threatened animal?
- Do you become tired all of a sudden?
- Do you become depressed? Do you feel like a deflated balloon?
- Do you become confused, perhaps feeling like you can't care for yourself?
- Do you feel like you don't belong?
- Do you become bored or stressed?
- Do you eat to excess?
- Do you judge others or take yourself too seriously?
- Do you drink, take drugs, or cut yourself?
- Do you shame or blame yourself, or do you blame others?
- Do you become discouraged and/or feel unworthy?
- Do you freeze with uncertainty?

Maybe you can't answer these questions yet, and that's okay too. This Mind Exercise will show you how to identify what happens in your inner world and outer world when you feel threatened. You'll uncover exactly which SELF you become when your primary SELF-defeating cycle arises, and you'll create an inner image to capture and tame it. You'll be ready to cope with the toughest moments you'll encounter along your final steps to Stillness.

WHY IT WORKS

SELF-defeating cycles are ingrained as cell networks in your inner world. Your brain has been structured to return over and over to producing this version of your SELF and the distracting inner world noise that it provokes.

As in Step 6, this mistaken SELF is not "you." It is an old brain-body habit. Over all the years of your life, your inner world has trained itself to recognize triggers as threats, and then to respond to some of the threats with a SELF-defeating cycle. The actual structure of your brain has settled into this habit and these patterns, which distract you from Silence.

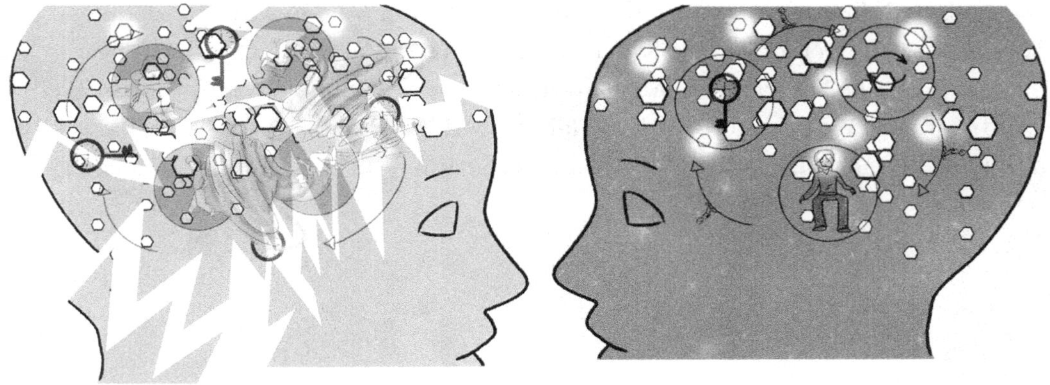

Old brain habits are reinforced by a SELF-defeating cycle, but new habits can be forged.

You have already started to build new patterns by making the Epic Shift when you recognize a key moment trigger event. Your brain's pathways are becoming ever more capable of reconnecting to Silence in the face of perceived threats.

The biggest obstacle, however, isn't the key moment trigger event that you identified in Step 6. It's yourself—or, more accurately, the version of your SELF that arises in a SELF-defeating cycle. Your Bridge of Translation has had years to perfect this SELF as an automatic, immediate response to potential dangers, and your cellular network has adapted to this. So much so that it's far too easy to assume that your reactions aren't even reactions; they're just "you being you."

But, again, this version of your SELF is an old reaction—both mentally and biologically—and this reaction can be stopped and transformed if you can master it. As you do so, you will change the actual biology of your brain, as brain science has shown, so that your automatic reactions no longer spark a SELF-defeating cycle, but a deeper connection to Silence.

RECONNECT TO SILENCE ALWAYS

That connection is your purpose. All you ever need to do to move forward on your path to Stillness, no matter how entrenched you may be in a SELF-defeating cycle, is to reconnect to Silence, listen, and be what you hear.

We all make bad choices. We get distracted away from being our purpose. We react habitually. We push too hard and fall down. Even inner world masters wander off their path. But the fundamental truth always remains—reconnecting to Silence brings us to our purpose.

Silence will always lead you to being your purpose.

It's that simple. Consistently quiet the noises your SELF produces, listen, and follow through on what you hear. Your connection to Silence will deepen, and your unique purpose will unfold through you.

Sometimes it takes time. I listened for years before I knew that my purpose called me to travel the outer world and write. I listened longer to understand exactly what the nature of that writing would be. And my purpose continues to unfold so long as I remain connected to Silence. That is what allows me to journey forward, ever closer to Stillness and living out my purpose.

And, just like me, even after you connect to Silence deeply, outer world voices—those of the ones you love or whose approval you seek—will attempt to distract you by demanding priority over Silence. You will wonder if you should listen to them rather than cultivating how Silence flows through you. These are forks in the path to Stillness, where you must make a choice. The choices you make determine who you will be tomorrow.

Choosing to listen to Silence will bring you ever closer to Stillness.

You can, however, return to those forks. I was shaken hard by the motorbike accident, and I took time to regroup. But I got back on the bike. And I made it to Pai.

I'll keep walking beside you too. The final steps of your journey must be made one hundred percent for you though. Unless you listen, hear, and see your SELF clearly in the key moments that provoke *your* SELF-defeating cycles, you'll frequently lose contact with Silence and get sidetracked from your journey. As we go forward on your epic journey, you must be aware and be committed. And remember: you always—*always,* no matter where you are in any moment—have everything you need to visit Stillness inside you right now.

Ready to face your primary SELF-defeating cycle?

Let's go.

THE DAILY RITUAL

Begin today's Mind Exercise by completing the Daily Ritual (starting with five minutes of physical exercise) located in Appendix A. When you have completed the Daily Ritual, return here to complete your Step 7 Mind Exercise. *You may access a video version of the Daily Ritual and Step 7 Mind Exercise at BeYourPurpose.com.*

Done with the Daily Ritual and ready to continue with your Step 7 Mind Exercise?

Good work. Let's keep going.

MIND EXERCISE

Identifying Your Biggest Obstacle

WELCOME TO YOUR STEP 7 MIND EXERCISE!

Explore the primary SELF-defeating cycle that unfolds in your inner world when a primary key moment trigger event slips past your awareness.

When you defined your primary key moment trigger event in Step 6, you began the process of identifying your primary SELF-defeating cycle. Review your list of key moment trigger events now, and write down your primary key moment trigger event here. (I've included mine below as well, so you can see my progression through this Mind Exercise.)

My Primary Key Moment Trigger Event

SEAN'S PRIMARY KEY MOMENT TRIGGER EVENT
Feeling lied to or abandoned

You will begin, in a minute, by consciously inviting your primary key moment trigger event into your inner world. Feel your inner world become uncomfortable. Notice the unpleasant feelings and associated thoughts arising in your inner world.

Do not shy away from this discomfort. You will be looking for the most persistent cycle of thoughts, emotions, and reactions that your primary trigger event provoked. Your goal is to observe the cycle that repetitively sabotages your connection to Silence—your primary SELF-defeating cycle. You may find that your primary SELF-defeating cycle was previewed in the Step 3 Mind Exercise, when you identified your resistance to being your purpose.

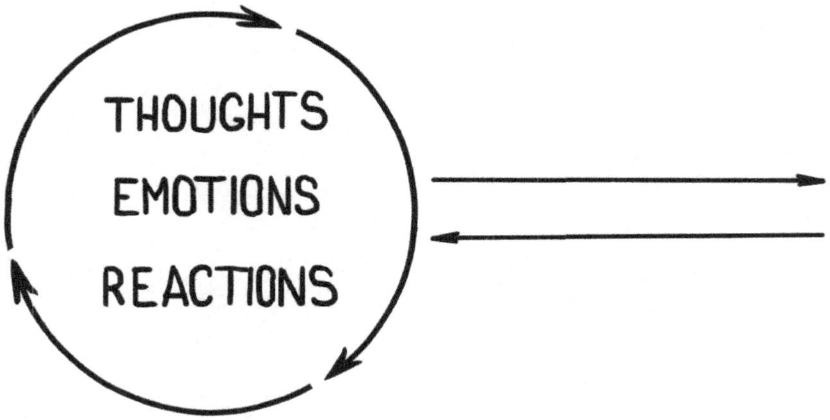

To fully define your cycle, become aware of what action(s) you typically take that either begin the cycle or exacerbate the experience. Because it's a cycle, the end of the cycle tends to perpetuate the beginning of the cycle into action again. And remember, sometimes an "action" is actually "inaction"—a failure to do something—that has the effect of perpetuating the cycle. (If that's hard to wrap your head around, think about going to the dentist. Someone who is scared of the dentist may put off making an appointment. The longer it's been, the harder it may be to call and schedule a visit. He may worry about the bad news he will hear, or that it will be even more painful to clean, or that the dentist will chastise him for being delinquent. The more time that goes by, the more those fears increase. Inaction perpetuates further inaction.)

Ready to observe your primary SELF-defeating cycle in your inner world?

Let's go.

When you're ready, follow these steps to identify your most pervasive patterns that distract you from Silence and being your purpose.

1. Take five conscious breaths to drop into the ocean of your mind.
2. Invite a memory of your primary key moment trigger event into your inner world to provoke your primary SELF-defeating cycle.
3. Close your eyes and observe your primary SELF-defeating cycle unfolding in your inner world. Consider how your primary SELF-defeating cycle has played out in your life before.
4. Open your eyes and write two sentences—using the format noted below and the example of my own primary SELF-defeating cycle that follows—to describe your primary SELF-defeating cycle as precisely as you can.

PRIMARY SELF-DEFEATING CYCLE FORMAT

Experiencing ____[your primary key moment trigger]___ causes me to feel ____[your feelings]___. This inner world sequence results in ____[your habitual reactions in a SELF-defeating cycle]___, which perpetuates the cycle in my inner world when ____[your reaction that primes you for repeating the cycle]___.

My Primary SELF-Defeating Cycle

SEAN'S PRIMARY SELF-DEFEATING CYCLE
Experiencing the possibility of being abandoned causes me to feel angry and scared. This inner world sequence results in me either becoming aggressive or withdrawing into inaction, which perpetuates the cycle in my inner world when I fail to communicate effectively with others or freeze rather than taking some action I want to take because I become scared of the possible consequences, often leading to others pulling away from me; I feel abandoned all over again, and the cycle repeats.

If you need more help uncovering your primary SELF-defeating cycle, you can add to what you've written after reviewing the "extra hints" at the end of this Mind Exercise.

Is your best first effort of unraveling your primary SELF-defeating cycle written down?

Good.

Now you'll capture your primary SELF-defeating cycle by choosing an imagined picture or scene that represents your primary SELF-defeating cycle.

Ready to visualize your primary SELF-defeating cycle?

Good.

Close your eyes and focus on an inner world image or movie of the SELF that you associate with your primary SELF-defeating cycle. Apply the most exaggerated image you can. Then, in the following space, describe and/or draw the image you've uncovered.

My Primary SELF-Defeating Cycle Image

SEAN'S PRIMARY SELF-DEFEATING CYCLE IMAGE
A scared little boy, uncertainly dipping one foot into a pool of water, then suddenly frozen still, unwilling or unable to move.

Got your image?

Excellent.

With the image in place, you can now master the inner world transition away from your primary SELF-defeating cycle.

This mastery begins by inviting your primary SELF-defeating cycle into your inner world again. I want you to actually see your primary SELF-defeating cycle image arising off your Bridge of Translation. Once you see it *and* feel it arising inside you, you will make the Epic Shift and reconnect with Silence.

When you're ready, begin by taking five conscious breaths to drop into the ocean of your mind. Then, close your eyes and reflect on your primary SELF-defeating cycle image over and over. Allow your SELF to feel the image—the unpleasant vibes, the fear, and the doubt associated with your primary SELF-defeating cycle. Allow your SELF to actually become the image.

The key right now is to feel this old SELF-defeating version of your SELF so deeply that you will always recognize it when it arises in the future.

Ready to become your primary SELF-defeating cycle image?

Go.

Feel it?

OK, good.

It's time to take inner world control. Make the Epic Shift to master your primary SELF-defeating cycle. Follow the three steps below now.

1. Recall your intention of making an inner world journey through Silence to Stillness.
2. Notice Silence flowing through your body.
3. Listen to your inner dialogue until it has quieted back into connection with Silence.

How does your inner world feel now?

Did you make the Epic Shift successfully? If your inner world still feels triggered at all by your primary SELF-defeating cycle, repeat the three steps to making the Epic Shift. You may need to repeat them several times for your inner world to feel calm again. That's okay. Take your time.

Feeling calm?

Great work!

You now know how to regain connection with Silence no matter what distracting influences arise in your inner world. As long as you make the Epic Shift, you can reconnect to Silence.

Don't worry if you are not convinced that you have fully uncovered your primary SELF-defeating cycle. Again, take your time. Follow the advice in the following section to refine what you've uncovered so far, and you *will* be able to master your primary SELF-defeating cycle.

EXTRA HINTS AND EXTRA PRACTICE

In Step 3, you may have gotten a glimpse of your primary SELF-defeating cycle when you committed one hundred percent to living fully up to your purpose. Your reaction in that Mind Exercise is often part of your primary SELF-defeating cycle.

Asking yourself certain questions can also help bring your primary SELF-defeating cycle into the light of inner world awareness. Honestly answer the following questions while noticing how intensely you feel provoked.

- Who in your life wounded you most and how?
- How do you respond to the wound that repeats in your life?
- From your perspective, what obstacles prevent you from living a life of great purpose?
- What is the most repetitive negative thought that has kept you from bathing in a peaceful Silence-centered state all the time?
- What belief might prevent you from visiting Stillness?

- What story do you become and what role do you play when you are provoked out of your emotional comfort zone?
- What is your biggest regret?
- What has been your most persistent inner world obstacle to progressing through *Be Your Purpose*?

Have you learned more about your reactions to triggers and habits that act as obstacles to your progress to Stillness? Keep any new discoveries in mind as you repeat this Mind Exercise from the beginning. You should continue to repeat the Step 7 Mind Exercise until you feel confident that you've defined your primary SELF-defeating cycle image and will notice it any time it arises as you complete your journey to Stillness. You may do this all right now, or you may choose to repeat the Mind Exercise another time.

You've completed Step 7.
Congratulations!

By uncovering, capturing, and provoking your primary SELF-defeating cycle—and then making the Epic Shift back into connection with Silence—you've taken another massive surge along your journey to Stillness. You're ready for Step 8, which takes us into Thailand's most mountainous region—the perfect setting for our final steps to Stillness.

I'll see you again when you're ready to continue.

STEP 8

Visiting Stillness' Backyard

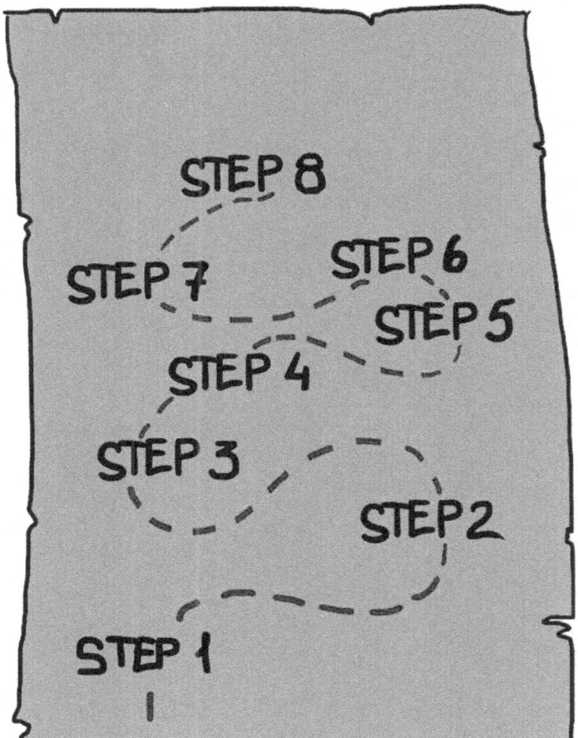

STEP 8: VISITING STILLNESS' BACKYARD

As the hand held before the eye conceals the greatest mountain, so the little earthly life hides from the glance the enormous lights and mysteries of which the world is full, and he who can draw it away from before his eyes, as one draws away a hand, beholds the great shining of the inner worlds.

—Rabbi Nachmann of Bratzlav

A winding four-hour ride through rainforests and mountain slopes brought me, finally, to Pai. In spite of no shared language, a traveling monk knew exactly what I sought. He pointed me to a remote valley under the stars where I spent the night in a bamboo hut.

Chiang Mai's city lights and sounds were far behind me. Silence flowed unmistakably through my new camp as the morning sun burst forth. I woke to acres of undulating rice fields, unfolding through the glistening valley leading up to still green peaks. So strong was the Silence, I was assured that I was on track, steadily moving away from stress. It was like being in Stillness' backyard.

The lush Silence pulsed through the mountains and flowed through me, allowing my mind to wander to one of my earliest memories of shifting versions of my SELF.

While bathing in Silence on my hut's porch, my mind wandered back to a vivid, life-altering dream I had about my grandmother, Nana, when I was seven. I hadn't recalled it in years.

Nana had always told me that a small mouse visited her every night, precisely at midnight. Oh, I wanted to believe this story. I could tell she wanted me to believe it, too. But I didn't. In my developing inner world, I had already formed categories of what was "possible." Mice visiting old ladies at precise intervals weren't among them. That, at best, would happen in a cartoon—and I knew those weren't possible either.

But my mind wasn't set in stone quite yet—maybe, just maybe, there could be something magical. So, while sleeping over at Nana's house, I asked if I could see the midnight mouse. Deep asleep by midnight I dreamt that Nana gently woke me and I sleepily followed her to the music room.

Side by side, we sat at the piano. Nana signaled me to be still with a single finger to her lips. Then, she began to play softly. Her long fingers flowed slowly, elegantly, up, down, back, forth, as though beckoning an honored guest. I relaxed into her, feeling completely at home as I rocked along to the melody.

After a minute, and without stopping the quiet song, Nana leaned down to my ear. "Shhh," she whispered to me. I looked up as she inclined her head towards the top of the piano.

A small mouse stood there, staring back at me. It should've been an exceptional sight, but it seemed entirely normal to me in that moment. I leaned back into Nana and watched her hands as she played for several more minutes. When I next looked up, the mouse was gone.

It was all so real to me. Wanting to believe Nana had changed what my mind produced. I had set my mind on a certain definition of what could be—my so-called reality. Nana had opened my eyes to the limitations of this mindset.

When I woke that morning, I told Nana I now knew the mouse was real. That night, Nana woke me just before midnight. We walked into the living room together and waited in front of the fireplace. When the clock struck midnight, a little, furry, brown mouse stepped forward. I rediscovered a child's eyes through which anything can and does happen.

As I returned my senses to the green Thai valley, I realized that, though unconscious to me at the time, this was perhaps my first experience of truly shifting my mindset. I could see how much that moment reopened my mind. Thanks to Nana, I learned that I could relinquish a SELF that limited me and my experiences.

MINDSET DICTATES EXPERIENCE

Isn't it fascinating that we have very concrete mindsets even at age seven? Even the word itself can be illuminating. The word itself means your beliefs and expectations, as well as the inner dialogue that these beliefs and expectations repeatedly provoke in your inner world.

But it also carries with it a rigidity. "My mind is set," people often say. Remember, your inner dialogue is programmed to be repetitive. The decisions you make today are determined in large part by inner dialogue that has long persisted in your inner world. Your *mind* is *set* by these patterns.

Your historical patterns of inner dialogue repetitively invite old SELF desires, judgments, and commentary. In many cases, these distract you from Silence. They color your choices and dictate your life experience.

Your mindset structures your brain and your very experience of life.

Brain science research has proven this. Your beliefs about the nature of the world structure your reality and, therefore, how you experience it. Have you ever heard the saying, "Can't means won't"? That's because your mindset—a SELF-defeating dialogue that refuses your ability—dictates your reactions and pretty much ensures that you won't do whatever it is. Mindset dictates experience.

SHIFTING MINDSET

It follows, then, that if we can shift our mindset, we can change our life experience. In fact, for seven steps, you've been working toward that. You have listened and watched with intention. You have created and shifted language and imagery using emotional visualization. Each step has changed your future because you are changing your mindset.

You now can remain aware of and consistently engage with the inner dialogue flowing off your bridge. You have learned how to produce new inner dialogue patterns—new mindsets. You no longer automatically default to a mistaken SELF; you are building new brain habits that enable more emotionally satisfying versions of your SELF for Silence to flow through. You are redefining how your brain and body will behave tomorrow.

The more intentional you can be in shifting mindset, the more strategically you can navigate to Stillness. New experiences become possible because you allow them to be.

It may help to think of old mindsets as heavy veils of fog in your inner world. These veils may cloak your view and disrupt your connection to Silence. But when you can shift the foggy veil of old mindsets, you clear the gateway to Stillness. To do so, you must clarify your beliefs and expectations, which rise off your Bridge of Translation like a calm breeze, removing the veils of fog and bringing your path into crystal clear focus.

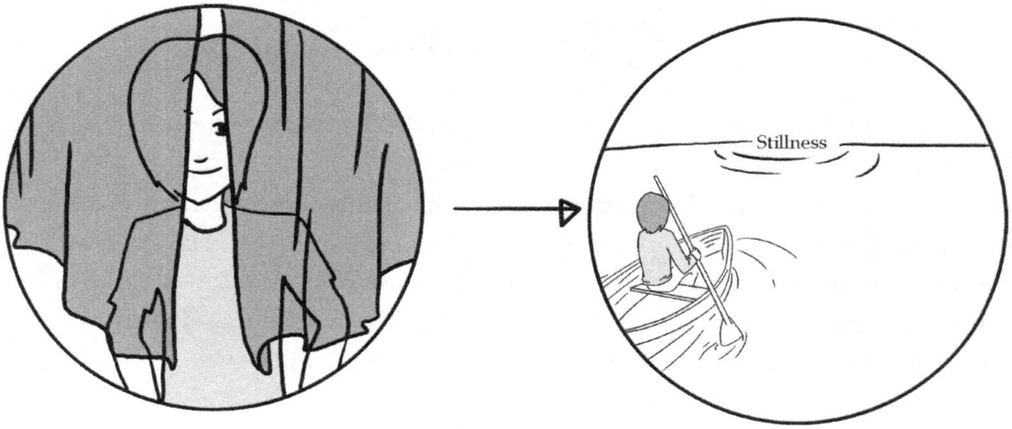

Shifting your mindset removes the veils that obscure the flow of Silence from Stillness.

This clarification is your next task. Just as the midnight mouse did for me, reconnecting to your belief in what can happen will shift your mindset so that you can visit Stillness' backyard today.

WHY IT WORKS

Science has proven that changes to your mindset change your physiology, your experience of everyday life, and even how your life unfolds. Ellen Langer, Ph.D., is a renowned Harvard University professor of psychology whose life work has shown this time and again.

Dr. Langer's research shows that the way people perceive their SELFs in relation to the world has significant impacts in their body, the outer world, and their future. In one landmark experiment, Dr. Langer demonstrated that if a person in his seventies behaves as though he is in his fifties, his physiology can change so completely that his body actually behaves in every way like that of a fifty-year-old.

Her years of work show that this kind of massive change is, in fact, typical of a shifted mindset. In other words, as written for one of her many awards for distinguished contributions, "Dr. Langer has demonstrated repeatedly how our limits are of our own making." And so, each time your brain makes the Epic Shift, your body and experience of life change entirely.

The power of this lies, in large part, in a clear and consistent intention, according to decades of brain science and psychology research. Dr. Langer and others have found that a deeply held mindset will produce and sustain greater brain and body changes. If you firmly believe that you'll arrive in Stillness, you'll strategically transform your inner world physiology into alignment with the outcome of visiting Stillness.

Today's Mind Exercise puts these psychology and brain science discoveries into practice in your life by fully aligning your mindset with your intention to visit Stillness.

BELIEVE IN YOUR JOURNEY

The breakthroughs and research on mindset have a key lesson in them: You must commit to and believe in your ability to journey to Stillness. Your commitment and belief combine to act as a North Star in your inner world, guiding you to your destination.

From today's Mind Exercise forward, you'll begin to notice a reduction in the traffic arising onto your Bridge of Translation. You may also notice a reduction in the intensity of the personal attachment you feel to the thoughts that do arise. These are some of the cumulative effects of your journey to Stillness.

Your power to intentionally slow your thoughts down has increased as well. When you habitually slow down the translation of inner dialogue on your bridge, you'll begin to feel far more relaxed throughout the day. Still, old brain habits can continue to make slowing your thoughts down a challenge.

This is when you must remember your commitment and belief.

Keep in mind, your SELFs can try almost anything to refuse to slow down. Once I observed an image of my SELF, sitting in a corner of my mind with crossed arms during Mind Exercise, softly muttering, "Fine!" under his breath. At first, I couldn't help but laugh at the sight of a SELF pouting about being asked to sit still for a minute. But as I laughed, I realized I'd fallen for another of the inexhaustibly creative tricks that old versions of my SELF employ. By getting me to laugh, he'd grabbed my inner world microphone back. I'd been distracted from my objective: quieting my mind.

Unceasing persistence and exceptional creativity are your SELFs' greatest assets for maintaining control of your bridge and, so, directing your attention away from

Silence. But if you maintain a belief in your ability to tame your SELFs into Silence, you will be able to slow your thoughts and shift your mindset to strategically enter Stillness' backyard.

Ready to deepen your connection to Silence and visit Stillness' backyard?

Let's go.

THE DAILY RITUAL

Begin today's Mind Exercise by completing the Daily Ritual (starting with five minutes of physical exercise) located in Appendix A. When you have completed the Daily Ritual, return here to complete your Step 8 Mind Exercise. *You may access a video version of the Daily Ritual and Step 8 Mind Exercise at BeYourPurpose.com.*

Done with the Daily Ritual and ready to continue with your Step 8 Mind Exercise?

Good work. Let's keep going.

MIND EXERCISE

Visiting Stillness' Backyard

WELCOME TO YOUR STEP 8 MIND EXERCISE!

Prepare your mindset to complete the journey to Stillness as we visit Stillness' backyard.

Visiting Stillness is possible when you expand your awareness of the broader life of which you are a part. You must connect to the knowledge that makes *you* most aware of life's miraculous nature—opening your mindset to the possibility of completing your journey to Stillness.

To shift your mindset to this extraordinary possibility, choose and write down five things that, to you, most clearly demonstrate the miracles of life. I call this list your everyday miracles.

Again, I've included my list below yours, so that you can see some of what guides me on my journey.

My Five Everyday Miracles

1. ______________________________

2. ______________________________

3. ______________________________

4. ______________________________

5. ______________________________

Sean's Five Everyday Miracles

1. An egg fertilizing, then its cells multiplying—leading to the birth of a newborn human baby
2. Transcendent art that flows through humans into the outer world
3. The replacement of every single cell in every human body every seven years while you remain "you"
4. Nana's "midnight mouse" appearing in my inner world
5. Billions of unified events unfolding inside me but outside my control each moment, animating one of the most complex embodiments in the known history of the universe: me

Done choosing your miracles?

Good!

By ushering your beliefs about the miraculous nature of life into your inner dialogue, you shift your mindset to deepen your connection to Silence. The deeper your connection to Silence, the closer you are to Stillness.

Slowly reread your five everyday miracles. Now, make the Epic Shift to further deepen your connection to the miraculous life flowing into you. Allow any arising inner noise, key moment triggers, or SELF-defeating cycles to quiet as you shift to a quiet inner world.

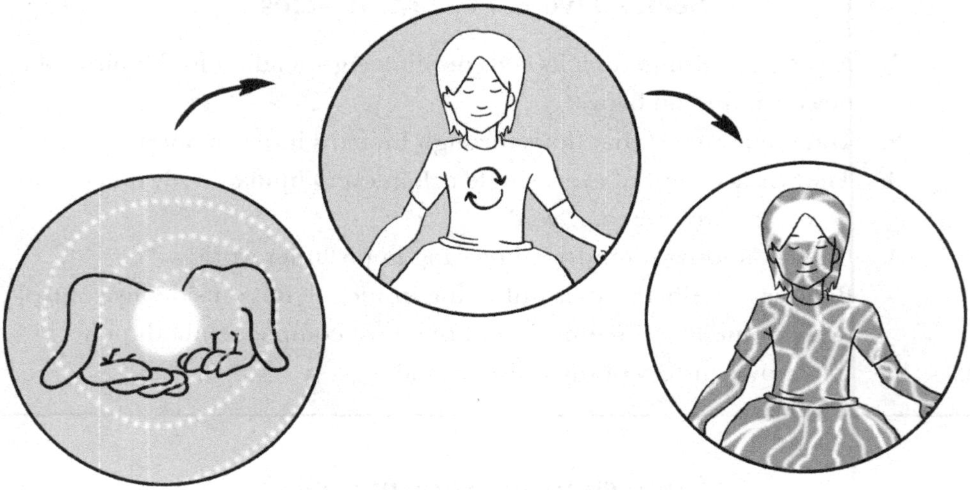

Did you read your everyday miracles and make the Epic Shift?

Feels good, right?

If your inner world is not tranquil, reread your list of everyday miracles and make the Epic Shift again. When all is quiet, you're ready to join me in Pai.

Emotionally visualize taking a stroll with me into the green valley in Thailand's lush mountain rainforest.

Look around and feel Pai's quiet, sprawling, day-lit landscapes arising in your inner world. Only the slow mountain breeze flows through this valley today. Together, we stand on the porch of the hut and allow Silence to encompass us. You are in Stillness' backyard.

As the sun goes down, however, the wind picks up. Clouds cover the moon, and sudden torrents of rain are unleashed. Silence roars to life. Thunderous bellows echo through your body, rousing your inner world into a palpable connection to Silence.

Jolted into awareness, you want—no, *need*—more. You want to be closer to Silence. We walk off the porch and into the drenching rain.

We stand in the cold rain of the night storm. Feel rain warming as it spills over your warm back, covering you, puddling below, soaking your mud-cloaked feet. You are enveloped in roaring Silence—a vertical river showering timelessness over you, through you.

Sink into the sense of Silence, deepening the connection. Your feet press into the ground, swallowed to the ankle. You are immersed in the relentless barrage of the night releasing. These are our brief moments lit by Silence, alive, shrouded beneath the storm-hidden infinite.

Look up at the sky above. Its vast, open space is shaded by clouds, hiding trillions of lights. The moon peeks through, and its light softens our dripping faces. Lose yourself in the white noise of Silence.

Do you feel it? Close your eyes and feel Silence pouring through you.

Ready to let roaring Silence consume you for one minute?

Go.

Feel Silence.

With the turn of the page, the downpour ends. The roar of Silence retracts to the infinite from which it fell. Life stills for a perfect instant.

Now.

Breathe.

Know that anything is possible in any moment listening to Silence. The world skips a beat before the creatures in waiting chorus back to life. Dripping, buzzing, ecstatic. Exhale hard with me to a world return to motion, a jungle rising in the dark, applauding, joining our gratitude for a visit to Stillness' backyard.

You've completed Step 8.
Congratulations!

You have intentionally navigated into Stillness's backyard. New experiences have become possible in your inner world, and you have a hint of Stillness tucked inside you.

I'll see you again when you're ready to continue.

STEP 9

Embodying Your Silence SELF

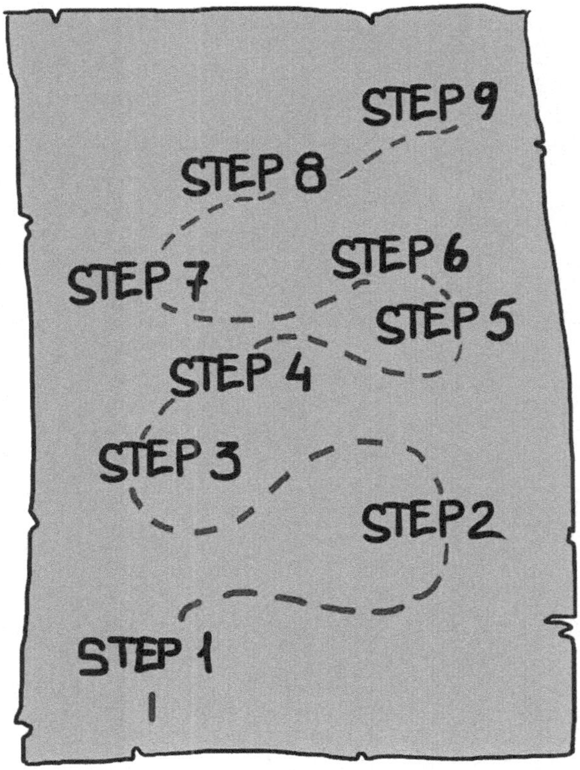

STEP 9: EMBODYING YOUR SILENCE SELF

No individual has any right to come into the world and go out of it without leaving behind him distinct and legitimate reasons for having passed through it.

—George Washington Carver

In Pai, I spoke sparingly. Over my days there, repetitive thoughts, outer world concerns, and former desires faded as a deepened connection to Silence expanded within. The uncertain small boy had been soothed. I could see my calmed inner world crisply. I heard the call to move onward.

On my last morning there, I woke to Pai's bright sun, did the Daily Ritual, and hopped on the motorbike to ride three more hours through Thai rainforests. I would go as far and high as the bike would take me into tightly packed mountains beyond the remote forest villages of the Shan Hills dotting the outskirts of Mae Hong Son—the City of Three Mists.

On my way, I stopped at a riverbank. Leaving the bike behind, I carved a narrow path through endless green life. At a nowhere oasis spotlighted by a sun shaft shining through a crack in the forest canopy far above, I spotted a stone seat at a crossroad in the river. Time faded away as I sat down on the glowing stone.

Sun streaks painted me into the mountain terrain, quieting my mind as my inner and outer world merged to the flow of Silence. I am insulated from the modern world by the dense forest and the knowledge that time flows to Stillness. The river's rush accompanied a grand symphony of creatures keeping perfect time together.

My mind wandered back fourteen years to California and my first visit to Stillness. I saw myself aching with a broken heart, beginning to slowly pluck a guitar on my lap. And I once again felt the miracle that surrounds and flows through us.

The vast miracle of life was so obviously apparent to me in that moment. Every cell of my being acknowledged that billions of unified events constantly unfold inside me, outside my control, and they animate the most complex embodiment of life in the known history of the universe: me, you, all of us. All questions and thoughts disappeared in me. My stilled mind joined Stillness.

Just as on my many other visits to Stillness, I heard the same message:

Just as you are making a journey through life…

...a silent energy of life is also making a journey through you.

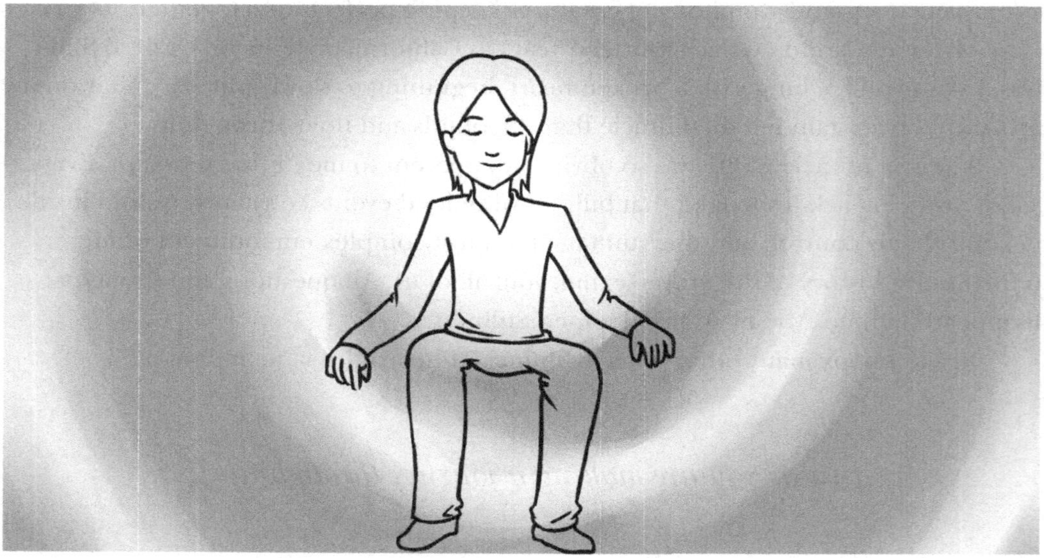

My connection to Silence was deep and true. I had embodied my Silence SELF.

YOUR SILENCE SELF

Science has taken us to the precipice. To bridge the remaining distance between your SELF and Stillness, you must actually experience yourself as part of the ongoing miracle that life is—you must embody your Silence SELF.

Throughout history, inner world masters have taught that deeply connecting to Silence produces a feeling of inner world harmony. The experience has also been described as feeling loved so thoroughly that you actually become one with love. You feel the embodiment of love for all life, including loving your SELF.

This experience arises as you deepen your awareness that the cells forming your brain, body, and thoughts are constructed of Silence. When you are deeply immersed in awareness of Silence animating you, you embody your Silence SELF.

The act of embodying your Silence SELF is not simply thinking about the idea of it. It is actually *experiencing* your Silence SELF. This is as different as imagining an abstract possibility in your future—perhaps musing, *Wouldn't it be nice to be in Paris in April?*—versus actually feeling and knowing something as *you*, right now—*I am sitting in a coffee shop and watching the sun stream through the windows.*

When you embody your Silence SELF, you fuse yourself to Silence. You acknowledge that you are made of Silence and that Silence is flowing through you. You feel the meaning with which Silence embues you, and you know you have the ability to direct its flow.

Remember: As it flows into you, Silence is constantly eliciting your response to the creative power it offers. By requiring and empowering the remaking of your SELF each moment, Silence infuses meaning into your life. When you listen closely, and strategically choose how Silence transforms as it flows through you, your choices take on great meaning—the crafting of the world we share.

> *The deeper your connection to Silence grows, the more you can hear, feel, direct and follow Silence as it flows through you to live your unique purpose.*

WHY IT WORKS

Dr. William James, widely considered the father of modern American psychology, reached beyond the vital idea of mindset that brought us into Stillness' backyard in Step 8. His research proved the qualitative difference that inner world content can bring to outer world life experience.

Dr. James studied the deep emotions that arise in concert with awareness of the miraculous nature of life, and he found that it opens a gateway to "transcendent" states often seen in saints and sages. He concluded that, when your inner world fills with enough love, indignation, generosity, loyalty, enthusiasm, admiration, or awe, your SELF's sense of independent importance diminishes. Your body then shifts into an extraordinary state of connected awareness. This is a state that you now know well—a deep connection to Silence.

Dr. James also found that those who experience a transcendent state (in his words) were more likely to put fewer limits on themselves and to experience an entirely different quality of life.

Over the last century, Dr. James' insights have sparked generations of theoretical development in psychology. Meanwhile, technological advances have provided modern scientists with a closer look at exactly how the human brain and body is equipped to produce the expanded states of experience that Dr. James observed and described. For example, we now know that each human brain cell is connected to an average of ten thousand other brain cells, creating a brain and body structure with over one million billion links.

We also know that your brain-body cell network enables you to process roughly eleven million bits of information per second. Meanwhile, you only have conscious access to roughly forty bits of information per second. We commonly refer to those forty conscious bits as our "attention."

Each step of your journey has cultivated your connection to Silence—the source empowering your inner world. You have become a master of using your forty bits of attention to listen to and direct more of the eleven million bits of information that your brain and body are processing each second of your life.

As Dr. James predicted, doing so has massively increased your inner world power. By taking control of directing your attention, you've changed your brain cells and grown new connections between brain cells. Meanwhile, by consistently making the Epic Shift you've been opening your gateway to Stillness.

In today's Mind Exercise, you'll strategically focus your forty bits of conscious attention to hear and direct your eleven million bits of inner world processing. You will continue changing the structure of your brain in order to open the gateway to Stillness.

FOCUS ON THE NOW

For eight steps, you've strategically increased your ability to make use of the massive power flowing through your inner world. Consistent practice has grown your inner world vision substantially. Your map to Stillness is nearly complete, and you can strategically navigate by following and transforming Silence as it flows within you. During these final days of our journey, your inner world should be primarily focused in the present moment.

Deeply connecting to Silence requires a crystal clear mind, unencumbered by thoughts of past, future, or outer world distractions.

Focus on the now in your inner world.

If you have not been focused on your inner journey, enjoying a quieted mind for the last twenty-four hours particularly, I suggest you cultivate a quieted inner world state for at least that period of time before moving forward.

You'll be moving into new territory as you access a new experience of your SELF. You will leave your day-to-day material life behind, moving outside of it to fully open your mind to the miracle occurring within you. When you look through the right lens, the vast miracle of which you are a part is revealed in everything. Your capacity to direct attention to your bridge can shift the flow of Silence through you and open a gateway within you.

As you listen in awe to purpose flowing though you, you'll inhabit a categorically different inner world—your Silence SELF. As your Silence SELF, you will take your next major step toward Stillness

Ready to embody your Silence SELF?

Let's go.

THE DAILY RITUAL

Begin today's Mind Exercise by completing the Daily Ritual (starting with five minutes of physical exercise) located in Appendix A. When you have completed the Daily Ritual, return here to complete your Step 9 Mind Exercise. *You may access a video version of the Daily Ritual and Step 9 Mind Exercise at BeYourPurpose.com.*

Done with the Daily Ritual and ready to continue with your Step 9 Mind Exercise?

Good work. Let's keep going.

MIND EXERCISE

Embodying Your Silence SELF

WELCOME TO YOUR STEP 9 MIND EXERCISE!

Deepen your connection to the miraculous reality surrounding and flowing through us. Embody your Silence SELF.

You should feel effortlessly connected to Silence as we begin this Mind Exercise. Your mind and mood should feel light, open, quiet, and singularly oriented to your inner journey. Strategically visiting Stillness occurs after you know yourself as an ongoing embodiment of the Silence flowing through you. So let's intentionally deepen our connection to the miraculous reality surrounding and flowing through us.

Be deeply aware of the separate nature of your inner world experience from your outer life situation—notice how the activity of observing, navigating, tending, and quieting your inner world is qualitatively distinct from pursuing the day-to-day details of your outer world life situation.

Let go of your outer world concerns.

Are you feeling at peace with life?

Good. Let's keep going.

Sit down beside me on our glowing stone seat at the river crossroad now, our backs facing the setting sun. Feel the day's last rays warm your skin as the mountain's jungle eases into night.

Feel Silence flowing effortlessly through you.

As though an invited visitor in Stillness' backyard, listen as your whole mind and body envelops into the grand symphony of untamed life pulsing through our glowing stone seat right now. Surrounded by the river's rush of Silence, accompanied by a billion creatures keeping perfect time together, be painted by the sun into the mountain forest. Your inner and outer worlds merge into one flow—Silence.

Make the Epic Shift to strategically connect to Silence. Take a deep breath with me.

Be quiet and feel your SELF as Silence. Feel your inner world infusing with Silence. Know your SELF is being created by the miracle of life flowing through you right now. Open your mind to the transcendent experience of knowing that your SELF is emerging from the flowing miracle that life is—Silence.

Become aware of your inner journey through Silence to Stillness. Subsume all inner noise in the infinite space of you. Feel Silence flowing as you listen to your quieting inner dialogue.

Let go of all judgment.

Disengage from fantasies of what today or tomorrow might bring.

Leave stories behind.

A quiet mind.

As we sit together on our glowing stone seat, our quiet minds connected to life's silent miracle flowing through us, orchestrating billions of synchronized events within and outside us each moment, invite your everyday miracles into your awareness. Listen; see them flowing over your bridge as you settle deeper into Silence.

Focus inside now. Listen, watch, feel Silence bursting, rushing unobstructed over your bridge. Be consumed in Silence flowing through you. You've been here before—immersed, feeling here right now, never rushed, where fear has no name.

Look closely inside and see your SELF flowing out of the miracle flowing through you and over your bridge. Feel the vast space in your stilling mind, seeing Silence gaining speed now, accelerating off your bridge out into limitless space, shattering the bonds in your inner world.

See Silence bursting through you.

Be nourished by it, nurtured. Be astonished and awed by Silence's unlimited flow, moving faster through the space in you. Allow your fusion to Silence to grow, unrestrained.

Set perfectly still on your stone seat, consumed by Silence pouring through you, watch as your bridge—your SELF—fades to transparent now. A translucent bridge transforming into flowing Silence.

Be the space of your inner world. Feel only Silence now. Connect fully.

Fuse with Silence. Close your eyes and know your SELF as Silence.

Be your Silence SELF for one minute.

Go.

Done with one minute?

Good job.

Invite the following question onto your bridge now. Be Silence for one more minute as you listen for hints of your unique purpose arising through you.

For what purpose is Silence flowing through me now?

Ready to close your eyes, invite the question onto your bridge, and listen for one minute?

Go.

Done with one minute?

Good.

In the space below, write down anything that arose through your Silence SELF. There are no wrong answers. And it all matters. Write whatever you experienced while merged with Silence.

Again, I've included my experience so that we can continue this journey side by side.

My Arising Purpose

> **Sean's Arising Purpose**
>
> To pour Silence artfully into the outer world by sharing what I learn about psychology, brain science, and inner world mastery.

Done?

Good job.

If you didn't hear anything that feels like your unique purpose, don't worry at all. Just as I did for years before hearing an outer world call, you'll keep listening. When you are connected to the peace of Silence and you are listening, you are being your purpose.

Listening as your Silence SELF energizes you, inspires you, and connects you to your unique life of purpose. When the time is ripe and you are listening, your unique purpose flows into inner focus and unfolds through you into the outer world.

You've completed Step 9. Congratulations!

You now can embody your Silence SELF whenever you choose. You are fully prepared to complete your journey to Stillness. Fantastic work!

But before you continue, I have a special message for you. Taking Step 10 to visit Stillness for the first time requires some special preparation, so please read carefully.

First, it's important to begin Step 10 with your mind and body immersed in connection to Silence. Be sure that you've been feeling calm and peacefully connected to Silence for at least 24 hours before you take Step 10. If you feel at all stressed, cultivate your connection to Silence by completing only the Daily Ritual on the day before you take Step 10.

Second, you'll need to plan where you want to be for Step 10. Choose an outdoors location where you'll feel completely comfortable and safe in the daylight. A beautiful park where you'll feel safe closing your eyes is a great choice. Or perhaps in a forest by a river. Ideally, find a stone seat where you can sit down comfortably. It's worth taking the extra time to find the perfect spot for you.

Third, come prepared for both comfort and connection. If it's going to be cold at all where you are, bundle up so you are comfortable. You should complete Step 10 while it's light out and wearing sunglasses. This is important.

Finally, if you've been reading your Mind Exercises, rather than listening to or watching them online, you may choose to continue reading straight through Step 10. If you've been listening to or watching your Mind Exercises, I suggest you wear headphones to complete your Step 10 Mind Exercise while sitting on your stone seat. Connect to your mobile device and listen. When it's time for your exercise before the Daily Ritual, pack your device away.

When you've completed your exercise, return to your stone seat and sit back down. Take a moment to feel Silence pouring into and through you, painting you into the world. Put your headphones back on or continue reading. You'll be ready to visit Stillness.

Got it?
Great!

I'll see you again when you're ready to visit Stillness.

STEP 10

Visiting Stillness

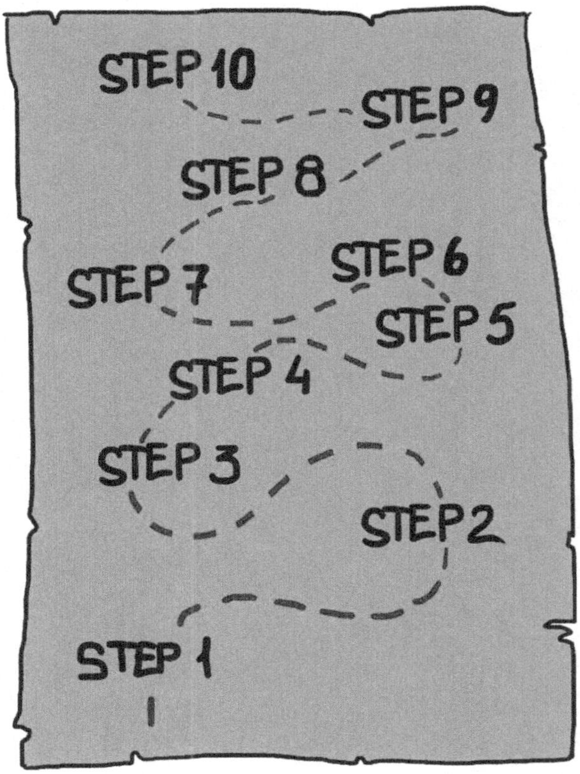

STEP 10: VISITING STILLNESS

The true monk, writes an Italian mystic,

takes nothing with him but his lyre.

—William James

A few days later, as the sun rose, I hiked back to the nowhere oasis. With my coffee in hand, I looked forward to settling into my Silence SELF on the stone seat again.

Two monks approached from the other direction. One stopped a few feet away. He motioned me to stop, then stared at me intensely for a few moments. He called his friend over. Smiling, he pointed at my neck.

The second monk's mouth opened slightly as he looked too. His eyes brightened, and he pointed to the same spot. The monks' smiles grew wide.

The first monk met my eyes with his deep brown ones, peering deeply for another long moment. Time slowed perceptibly. He nodded deliberately at my neck. Instinctively, I invited him closer.

Reaching forward, he closed two fingers, peeling something away from just below my right ear. I stared as he slowly opened his hand. A mature pupa pulsed restlessly in his palm—a former caterpillar opening in its cocoon, completing its transformation.

"Turning to butterfly," the first monk said.

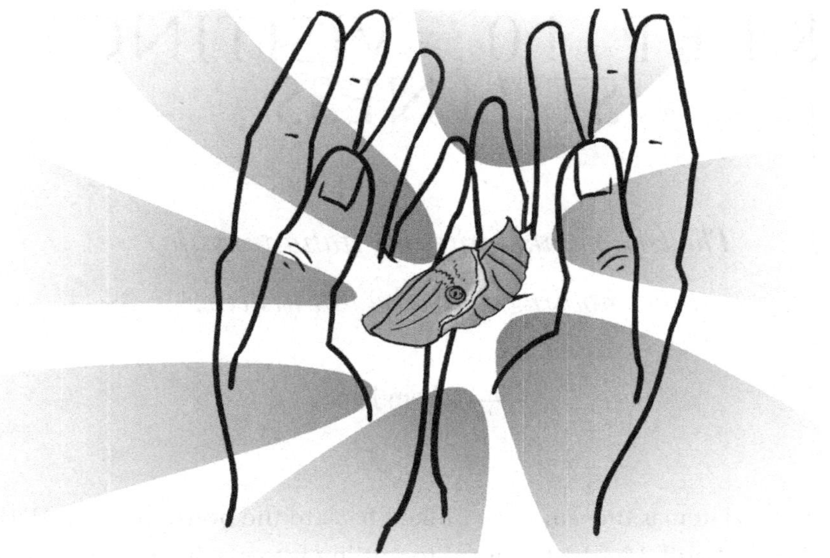

We watched together as new life emerged. Wings filling, slowly opening, transparent perfection taking flight in a brand new world. A butterfly was born.

Born anew ourselves we three witnesses smiled Silence. My brief friends then bowed deeply, turned, and continued along their path, just as we now turn to take the final step along ours.

TIME AND THE INNER WORLD

Your conscious thoughts mark time (in the inner and outer worlds). By processing information into thoughts in your inner world, your Bridge of Translation chops the information that flows onto it into chunks of time. This activity produces your experience of things being separate from one another—a time-bound experience wherein you are separate from the rest of life as it moves piecemeal through time.

When thoughts don't emerge onto your bridge, however, they don't create time inside you either. Instead, you experience a different reality than the time-bound experience your SELF renders. You experience your body, your thoughts, and your SELF existing as one with Stillness. When flow of Silence stills in you, you become one with the grounding from which everything that becomes separate emerges.

TIME SLOWS TO STILLNESS

As we've journeyed together, you've learned how to quiet the inner world activity of your SELF. Whenever you choose to, you can diminish the intensity and frequency of the thoughts arising in your inner world. You have developed the capacity to slow—and, soon, to stop—inner world time.

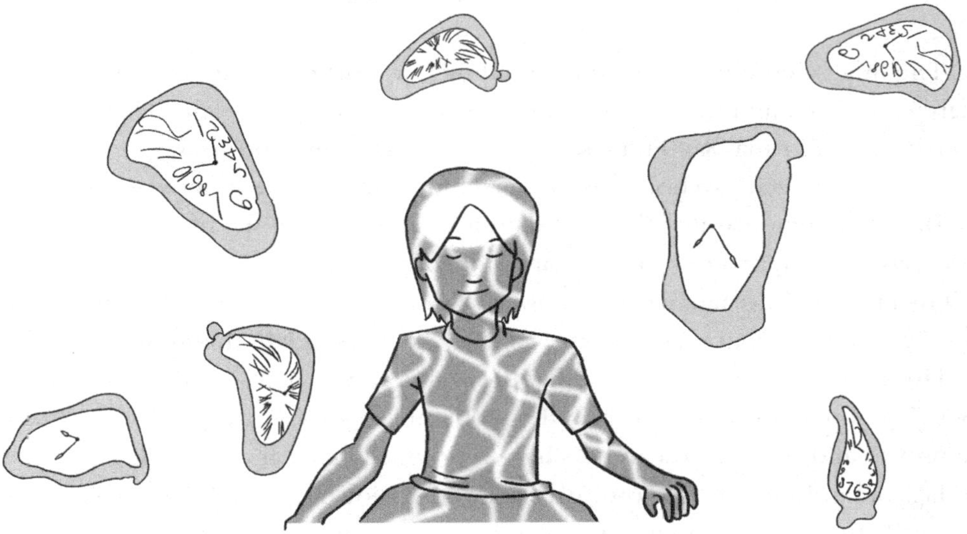

When you slow your inner dialogue and thoughts, you limit the concept of time in your inner world. Inner time slows down as you quiet your mind. The ideas that create and maintain your Bridge of Translation fade from your imagination.

When that happens, you experience Silence more and more expansively because the Silence flowing through you is less sequenced by markers of time—your thoughts. When you are able to do this completely, time will stop for you, and you will merge into Stillness. You will enjoy a rarefied, uninterrupted, unparalleled non-experience. Your conscious and unconscious worlds, unburdened by time, will align into perfect synchronicity with one another.

Now, at the final step to Stillness, you can and will achieve this.

Plucked from time's duality to commune in the singular harmony of being, your inner world functions overlap, drawing you out of time into Stillness.

WHY IT WORKS

The final scientific breakthrough guiding our journey to Stillness brings us full circle, back to San Francisco, California, where my journey began. There at the University of California, San Francisco, Dr. Benjamin Libet conducted groundbreaking research that changed psychologists' understanding of how the inner world operates.

Dr. Libet demonstrated that our actions do not begin at the moment we perceive our decisions to act, and our thoughts are not consciously produced in the moment. We all feel that we have agency—the power to choose our behavior in any moment. It seems that, when we make a decision to act, we are making it in that moment.

However, Dr. Libet discovered that the decisions we "make" and actions we "choose" are not made consciously in the moment we perceive they happen. Instead, as he proved and as many researchers have reproduced in years since, the conscious mind lags behind the unconscious. We are not consciously aware that we have begun to act until after our unconscious minds initiate the action.

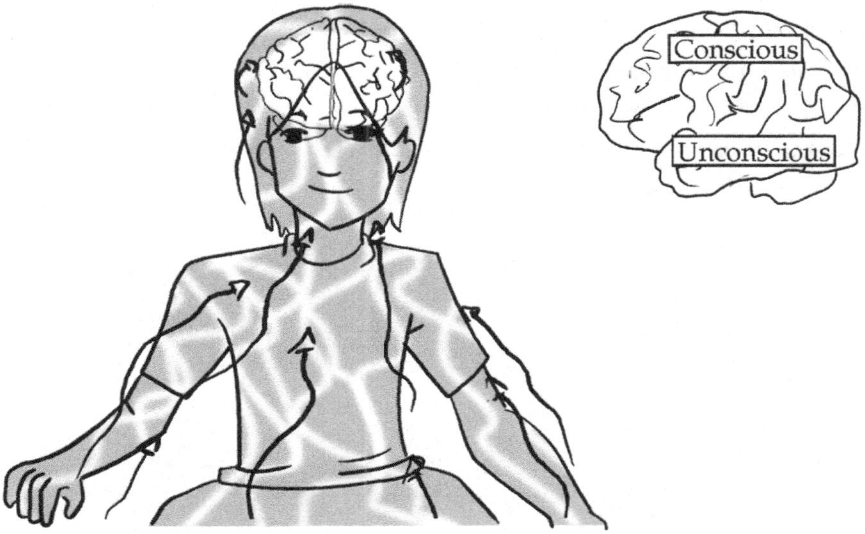

Silent energy activates inner world activity that your conscious awareness only later joins.

We do not feel this time lag, though—we feel like we consciously initiate actions. Our minds uphold this illusion by "backward time-stamping" everything we become consciously aware of. This backward time-stamping occurs automatically, out of our awareness, and creates the impression that we are making our choices in each moment.

When you can eliminate the brief delay required by this time-stamped chase and by the time-bound inner world it reconstructs and renders, you can commune uninterrupted with unchanging Stillness. You remove the construct of time and merge into Stillness.

COMMIT TO AND BELIEVE IN YOURSELF

When you are freed from your SELF, your mind will quiet completely. Guided primarily by the unequivocal intention you've instilled in your inner world throughout your journey, Silence will then slow to the precipice of Stillness. Your unwavering belief in yourself as being ready to follow Silence to Stillness is then your final step.

Infused in Silence, we'll navigate to a truth discovered outside time-bound opinions, in a state of wholeness that can't but instill your body with meaning from beyond relativity—the only way underived purpose could ever reveal itself to you. Your SELF will disappear as you effortlessly transform. Free from the world of concrete forms, your inner world will dissolve into the wholeness of being—Stillness.

When you know yourself to be connected to all of existence, your eyes begin to see a world of connections. Rather than experiencing yourself as separate, bound by time, body, mind, and place, you experience a timeless whole where you are always connected and never alone.

In your inner world, your perspective of distance, time, and space are your own to create. Your inner world is always one step from Stillness.

With each step to Stillness, your brain and body have changed. You've observed your key moment triggers that distracted you from listening to Silence and being your purpose. You've navigated through your inner obstacles and embodied your Silence SELF. You've sat in Silence flowing through you.

Having taken each step you are now perfectly prepared to visit Stillness. The depth of your visit will correlate to the clarity of your awareness of yourself as miraculous and worthy—as Silence returning to Stillness.

You have altered cellular structures that Silence flows through. By changing your inner world you have changed how your SELF can see, understand, experience, and relate to the world. Like a caterpillar emerging as a butterfly, you're now ready to experience a new world.

Today you'll dissolve the final inner veils separating you from Stillness.

Let's go.

THE DAILY RITUAL

Before you begin, remember that Step 10 is best done in an outdoor location where you'll feel safe. If you can find a stone seat in the sun, that is ideal. Wear sunglasses and clothing that will be comfortable.

Begin today's Mind Exercise by completing the Daily Ritual (starting with five minutes of physical exercise) located in Appendix A. When you have completed the Daily Ritual, return here to complete your Step 10 Mind Exercise. *You may access a video version of the Daily Ritual and Step 10 Mind Exercise at BeYourPurpose.com.*

Done with the Daily Ritual and ready to continue with your Step 10 Mind Exercise?

Let's visit Stillness.

MIND EXERCISE

Visiting Stillness

WELCOME TO YOUR STEP 10 MIND EXERCISE!

Take your final step and visit Stillness.

For nine steps navigating our inner worlds together, we've journeyed around the outer world's living history of psychology, brain science, and inner world mastery. Doubts, fears, and inner noise have silenced. Arriving now at our nowhere oasis, let's settle into our glowing stone seat and complete our journey.

Leaving outer world remnants, expectations, and time itself behind, we'll follow our journey to its ultimate destination—Stillness.

Together on our glowing stone seat again, surrounded by the density of life at the mountain river crossroad, hold only your intention to still the Silence flowing through you. Recall your intention of making an inner world journey through Silence to Stillness. Notice Silence flowing through your body. Listen as your inner dialogue quiets into the flow of Silence moving through you.

Be Silence.

Know nothing is missing here. Make the Epic Shift again now by silently saying to yourself, "I am going to visit Stillness now." Remember that the real journey of our lives is occurring inside us in this moment. Feel Silence flowing through you. Truly feel Silence vibrating within you.

Do you truly feel Silence?

Good.

Listen now as your mind quiets fully into connection to Silence. Feel Silence deeply. If you become distracted from your intention to visit Stillness anytime, just return here where nothing is missing to begin again by making the Epic Shift.

Connected to all that surrounds us by a silent miracle flowing through everything, intentionally embody your Silence SELF. Know your SELF as Silence now—be aware, feel, become the flow of Silence roaring through your body, over your Bridge.

Remember. You've been here before—where fear has no name. Feel the vast inner space of Silence flowing, accelerating, gaining space inside you. Be nourished, nurtured, astonished, awed in Silence's gathering, channeled untamed through you. Cherish your fusion to Silence.

Set still on our stone seat, consumed by Silence pouring through you, see your bridge creating your SELF growing translucent—transparent. Transform your SELF to Silence now. See, hear, become Silence.

Offer no resistance. Just relax. Keep watching. Take a deep breath. Let your shoulders relax toward the ground. Only watching and listening to Silence, right here, right now. Immerse completely into Silence lighting your inner world.

Watching the flow inside you is getting in touch with what you fundamentally are: Silence flowing into and through you.

Close your eyes. See and feel your whole body in Silence.

Embody your Silence SELF for one minute.

Go.

Feel Silence flowing effortlessly through you.

Done with one minute as your Silence SELF?

Good job. Let's visit Stillness.

Be yourself as timeless perfection connected to everything now. Release any lingering thoughts, judgments and attachments. Remain fully relaxed and fearless as you merge to Stillness for as long you desire.

Place your full attention into each word now. Read slowly. Recognize Silence flowing through the words, just as Silence flows through you.

Silence animating your cells animates these letters. Silence animates inner and outer worlds, and Silence is the space between. Complete immersion in this awareness stops time—dissolving SELF to Stillness.

Embody truth. Be Silence flowing through your stone seat now, into and through your body, filling you, pouring out in front of you, lighting more and more within and around you. Silence pours into the world around you, into the colors and scents and textures. Silence flows through each as through you.

Remove your sunglasses and set them beside you now.

See the light of Silence pouring in, lighting you from the outside too. Your inner and outer worlds are fully lit in the warm light of Silence, rivers of Silence meeting, converging, brightening, smoothing your view.

Stay relaxed; focus on Silence, these words, the surrounding beauty, the light inside your mind, the inner and outer converging to one.

See bright light wrapping all around you now. Silence lighting from all sides, inside and outside, cradling you, brightening everywhere.

Now, feel. Feel light filling your entire body. Feel light as your body connected to your world. Silence fills you always. Feel immersed in Silence growing in your body, filling your body, connecting you to everything.

Feel Silence as brightness flowing in everything, everywhere, and within you—this is you. Smile a world of Silence.

The deeper you feel and see Silence, the slower Silence flows. Feel, see, be only Silence, slowing now.

Slower and slower and slower.

Slower and slower and slower.

Relax into it further, approaching nothing.

Slower and slower and slower.

Close your eyes, finally, to Stillness.

You did it.

You stopped inside time, a perfectly still mind as one with the distant peaks, breathing, tasting the slow breeze.

Time is returning—a river of Silence flowing back into SELF. Go slowly. Savor. Spend the night immersed.

I'll meet you on our glowing stone seat one last time when you're ready.

BEING YOUR PURPOSE

Our destiny is to experience human life.

Our opportunity is to become our purpose.

CONGRATULATIONS!

You made your journey to Stillness and returned.

Whenever you want to see, hear, feel, know, be, remember, or leave your SELF behind, come back and sit in our glowing oasis. I'll return too, to relive our journey and remind myself how much our adventure to Stillness mirrors and informs the journey of our lives.

We are born into a human body and discover our SELF. We become aware of the stress-prone nature of our life's adventure. We journey through the ups and downs of a time-bound human world. In time, we return to timelessness.

By intentionally visiting Stillness during your life you return to your body flooded in Silence and embody a deepened awareness of the miracle our human journey is. Awareness of your own miraculous nature shifts from an idea into a truth residing in the cells of your brain and body.

Each time you visit Stillness your inner world focus will sharpen, and you'll see more clearly through the illusion of feeling separate from life itself.

Even after visiting Stillness though, human life requires you to confront its time-bound realities. Living in a physically separated and aging body sometimes provokes feeling incomplete, stoking unconscious and conscious fear, anxiety and inner struggle. Either you listen to your inner world, or you endure the consequences that arise when you disconnect from Silence.

Remember: Consistent connection to Silence can take years. Your persistent inner dialogue will arise and distract you from living your purpose. We have made this journey together to help you avoid the same mistakes that I made on my decades-long journey to being my purpose. You have already mastered looking inward to see the repetitive patterns you express, so you can shift away from them.

Right now, you may feel like everything has changed and is changing. That's how I felt when I first visited Stillness: My decisions changed, my priorities changed, how I experienced and interacted with others changed. An ever-new experience of life emerged. I felt peaceful, loving, caring, and young—fearless again.

I've lost my way from time to time since, and you may too. But whenever we visit Stillness, we deepen our embodiment of the truth: Although my life is not perfectible, always happy, or fully understood, it is perfect nonetheless. We are temporary, separate, vulnerable, and imperfect, *and* perfected Silence flows through us each moment.

By deepening your awareness of Silence—your inherent connection to the miracle of which you are a part—you transcend fears and pains emerging from the imperfection your temporary life situation implies. Each time you journey to Stillness, or even take a moment to make the Epic Shift, you claim freedom from the bonds of time.

Visiting Stillness and listening strategically actually grows you happier, healthier, kinder, more loving, more compassionate, more empathic—more reverent of others even. There is nothing more human, or more miraculous, than your capacity to observe, navigate and change the content, function, and structure of the cells of your own brain and body.

The convergence of neuroscience and inner world practice has demonstrated the power of prioritizing your awareness of Silence flowing through you to be your purpose. When you embody our shared mystery you co-create our shared world and live an unceasing revelation of purpose.

If right now is not perfect to you, make the Epic Shift. Your body comes to life—abuzz in Silence. Listen. It's remarkable.

When your inner space clears the content that distracts your awareness of Silence, you become your purpose. Everything and everyone you touch feels the peace and joy flowing through you. This is enlightenment—a light shining so bright awakens the world.

Thank you, Marta, Abigail and Jana for helping shine light through me.

A BRIEF AFTERWORD

It's been my privilege to walk the path to Stillness with you. Since returning to San Francisco, I've resumed my life as a psychologist, enriched and reignited—as flooded as ever in Silence from our journey to Stillness—to purpose.

I'd love to hear about your experience and stay in touch too. I set a page up *IJustFinishedBeYourPurpose.com*, so we can stay connected. I cordially invite you to drop by and say hello anytime.

My best always,

Sean

APPENDIX A

The Daily Ritual

Begin the Daily Ritual with a minimum of five minutes of physical exercise. Any physical exercise is fine; the important part is to get your heart rate elevated for at least five minutes. When you've completed your exercise, find a safe, comfortable space to sit down and complete the Mind Exercise sequence that follows.

Ready to raise your heart rate to prepare for the Daily Ritual?
Go.

Done with at least five minutes of exercise?

Good work.

Now, let's Mind Exercise and navigate to your Bridge of Translation so you can listen to the translation of your inner dialogue. Then, at the end of your Mind Exercise you'll deeply connect to Silence.

To begin, sit comfortably and focus all of your attention on sensing the tingling occurring in your body right now. I want you to focus on simply feeling how alive your body is.

Take a moment first to digest exactly what I'm asking you to do. You possess the ability to place your conscious attention directly *into* any specific location in your body that you choose, and you can sense the precise sensations, tingling, heat, energy—the silent energy of life that we call Silence—flowing into that specific location of your body this very moment.

Placing your attention into a part of your body to notice how it feels is such a routine task that you usually take your ability to do it for granted. Right now though, I want you to honor this superpower for the miraculous gift that it is. You are intentionally and strategically developing your capacity to access this inner world navigation tool.

As you improve your ability to place your conscious attention into your inner world to sense and connect to the Silence flowing through you, you'll notice that your entire body actually buzzes or tingles all the time. When you can focus all your attention only in your body, you can feel it abuzz with life. Placing your complete attention into your body connects you to an incredible feeling of aliveness.

This feeling is an aspect of Silence flowing into and through you.

Now, softly press the heel of your right foot down on the big toe of your left foot, then release the pressure on your left big toe. Focus all your attention on sensing the tingling that occurs as the blood rushes in. Feel it?

After you've felt the tingling for a few seconds, begin to move your attention to notice the tingling in different areas of your body. For example, shift your attention to the tingling in the other parts of your left foot. After a bit, notice how the tingling feels in your ankle, then in your calf.

Slowly move your attention up your leg and around your body as you choose, always focusing on the tingling sensation. If you get distracted during this task, just acknowledge what distracted you and then return your attention to where you left off.

Don't judge yourself for losing attention. Each time you notice that you became distracted and return your focus to your body, you are training your attention and your brain to perform at its best—you are taking a small step toward your intended destination: Stillness.

Close your eyes now and notice the subtle tingling in different areas of your body for two minutes.

Ready to close your eyes and notice your body's genius for two minutes?

Go.

Two minutes

Done with two minutes?

Good job. Let's keep Mind Exercising.

Now, listen to each sound you hear, especially sounds that normally go unnoticed. Allow your attention to move around the outer world—the world that exists outside your brain and body. Perhaps your attention will bounce from listening to a car moving toward and then driving away, or maybe you'll hear birds chirping. I want you to notice any sound that usually hums along without notice.

Without agenda, simply listen by placing your conscious attention into a state of open receptivity to whatever sounds arise in the outer world. When you listen intensely, you may begin to hear the world's pulse beneath the vibrating sound that arises—this pulse is Silence flowing through the outer world, all around you.

As before, if your attention has wandered, take note of what distracted you and then return your attention to listening. Don't judge yourself. Every return to attention is a small step toward your destination—you are training your brain and body to navigate your journey to Stillness.

Ready to close your eyes and listen for two minutes?

Go.

Done with two minutes?

Good job. Let's keep Mind Exercising.

So far you've shifted your attention from your inner world to the outer world. Now I want you to shift your attention solely to the air that comes into your body and leaves your body. Notice as it brushes against your nostrils and fills your lungs. Place your full attention into your breath—a conduit between your inner world and the outer world.

As you observe, allow your breath to grow deeper, bringing your attention to the calm depths of the ocean beneath your Bridge of Translation. Breathe in and out comfortably, with all of your attention on the flowing air that sustains your life, allowing your breath its natural desire to grow deeper and slower with each breath—in and out.

If you notice your attention has wandered anytime, just acknowledge what distracted you, what thought arose in your inner world. Return your attention to noticing your breath, and don't judge yourself. Each time you return your attention, you are navigating your journey to Stillness.

Ready to close your eyes and notice only your breath for two minutes?

Go.

Done with two minutes?

Good job. Let's keep Mind Exercising.

In the last minutes, you shifted your attention from your outer world—the world that exists outside your brain and body—to your breath, a conduit between your outer world and your inner world.

Continue now by shifting your attention to observing ideas arising in your inner world—your thoughts. I want you to move your attention toward where these thoughts emerge. This is your Bridge of Translation, where you can observe how the silent life energy that flows through you—Silence—is translated into the ongoing conversation that takes place inside your head. Follow these steps to find your own bridge and continue building a map of your inner world.

First, be open to the sense of emerging thought. Orient your attention on the space within you into which they arise. Second, shift your attention to observing the emerging thoughts. You may have to wait patiently for a thought to appear. When it arrives, know you have discovered the location of your Bridge of Translation. Third, note its location on your own inner world map.

Observe your Bridge of Translation, off of which all your thoughts and ideas flow.

Listen to and watch the translation of Silence into your thoughts and your SELF, flowing off your bridge. Notice the first thought arise and fade away. Then, notice the next thought that arises and fades away.

If you notice that your attention wandered during this task, perhaps being carried away into a stream of your thoughts—a developing inner movie—just direct your attention back to observing the thoughts flowing off your Bridge of Translation. Again, don't judge yourself. Each time, you are training your brain and body to navigate your journey to Stillness. You are taking a small step toward your destination.

Ready to close your eyes and visit your Bridge of Translation and listen for two minutes?

Go.

Done with two minutes?

Great work! Let's keep Mind Exercising.

Now I want you to experience your entire body tingling or buzzing. Shift your attention away from your thoughts and into feeling the Silence flowing through your entire body. Just as you noticed tingling in specific areas of your body before, feel Silence flowing now.

Once you connect to Silence, become aware of the precise sensations, instincts, intuitions, or impulses arising in your inner world. For example, you may notice arising impulses such as thirst, hunger, lust, sleepiness, or boredom.

If you sense anything arising through the buzz of Silence, just feel and listen. Observe the influence on your inner world. Do not seek to gratify the impulse. Simply become aware of the sensation for a moment. Then let it go, and reconnect to Silence.

Maybe something you experience is trying to speak to you, like an intuition. Just listen to your inner world. Then let it go as you reconnect to Silence.

Ready to close your eyes and feel Silence flowing through your entire body, to notice sensations, impulses, intuitions, and instincts arising in your inner world for one minute?

Go.

Done with one minute?

Good job.

You have completed the Daily Ritual.

APPENDIX B

Why Physical Exercise Matters

WHY EXERCISE *BEFORE* MIND EXERCISE?

The Daily Ritual begins with doing a minimum of five minutes of physical exercise of your choice.

There are plenty of good reasons to exercise before you Mind Exercise. For example, just five minutes of jogging per day has been found to reduce your risk of death by 30 percent. Also, for many people, the flow of Silence is much easier to sense and connect to immediately after exercising. But the main reason—the scientific foundation for exercise before Mind Exercise—is that exercise stimulates brain cell growth.

Dr. John Ratey from Harvard Medical School has shown that exercise actually generates the production of a protein in your brain called BDNF. BDNF, which stands for brain-derived neurotrophic factor, causes *new* brain cells to grow. It's been dubbed a master molecule and referred to as "Miracle-Gro for the brain" by Dr. Ratey.

Dr. Ratey calls BDNF "a crucial biological link between thought, emotions, and movement." BDNF binds to receptors in the synapses between neurons in your brain, increasing voltage (yes, your brain is electric!) and improving signal strength. Inside the cells, it activates genes that increase production of more BDNF and other important proteins as well as serotonin, the neurotransmitter vital for learning and self-esteem. Low levels of BDNF have been associated with depression and even suicide.

Basically BDNF improves the function of neurons, encourages new neurons to grow, and protects them from stress and cell death. Sprinkled on neurons in a petri dish, BDNF is observed to cause brain cells to sprout the structural branches required for learning—sort of like fertilizer for the brain.

How do you get more BDNF? You guessed it...

EXERCISE!

In this way, exercising primes you to get far more benefit out of completing activities like Mind Exercise. Getting your heart rate up before you Mind Exercise will accelerate your journey to Stillness.

REFERENCES

Brefczynski-Lewis, J. A., A. Lutz, , H. S. Schaefer, , D. B.Levinson, , & R. J. Davidson. (2007). Neural correlates of attentional expertise in long-term meditation practitioners. *Proceedings of the National Academy of Sciences, USA*, 104, 11483–11488.

Duck-chul Lee, PhD, et. al. (2014). Leisure-Time Running Reduces All-Cause and Cardiovascular Mortality Risk. *Journal of the American College of Cardiology.*

Ratey, J. *Spark.* Little, Brown and Company (January 10, 2008).

Langer, E. (2007) Mind-Set matters. exercise and the placebo effect. *Psychological Science* 18 (2): 165-171. And see, Langer, Ellen (2009). C*ounter clockwise: Mindful health and the power of possibility.* Place: Random House Publishing Group. And see, Langer, E. (1989). *Mindfulness.* Cambridge, MA: Perseus Books Group. See also, Dweck, Carol (2006). *Mindset.* New York: Ballantine Books. 7.

James, W. *The Varieties of Religious Experience: A Study in Human Nature. Being the Gifford Lectures on Natural Religion Delivered at Edinburgh in 1901–1902* (paperback), Classics. 2010.

Benjamin Libet, Unconscious Cerebral Initiative and the role of conscious will in voluntary action. Behavioral and Brain Sciences. (8) 533. 1985.

Made in the USA
Monee, IL
09 November 2026

68272530R00162